THE SUCCESS FANTASY

The Success Fantasy

TONY CAMPOLO

KINGSWAY PUBLICATIONS
EASTBOURNE

Unless otherwise indicated, biblical quotations are from the
New American Standard Bible © The Lockman Foundation 1960, 1962,
1963, 1968, 1971, 1973. Use is also made of the following:
KJV – King James Version, Crown copyright.
NIV – The New International Version © 1973, 1978, 1984 by the
International Bible Society.
PH – The New Testament in Modern English by J.B. Phillips,
© J.B. Phillips 1958, 1960, 1972.

ISBN 0 85476 497 6

Produced by Bookprint Creative Services
P.O. Box 827, BN21 3YJ, England for
KINGSWAY PUBLICATIONS LTD
Lottbridge Drove, Eastbourne, E Sussex BN23 6NT
Printed in Great Britain

Contents

1

What Is Success?

Success is a shining city, a pot of gold at the end of the rainbow. We dream of it as children, we strive for it through our adult lives, and we suffer melancholy in old age if we have not reached it.

Success is the place of happiness. And the anxieties we suffer at the thought of not arriving there give us ulcers, heart attacks, and nervous disorders. If our reach exceeds our grasp, and we fail to achieve what we want, life seems meaningless and we feel emotionally dead.

Since failure is our unforgivable sin, we are willing to ignore all forms of deviance in people if they just achieve the success symbols which we worship. Therefore, while we send those guilty of petty crimes to prison, we honour our robber barons by calling them *philanthropists*.

What is success? The word means many things, but for the sake of our discussion, let us agree that in our culture *success* means an individual has gained for himself one, if not all, of the following: wealth, power, and prestige. Sociologists teach us that wealth, power, and prestige express a 'strain to consistency'. This means that when people possess one of these, they tend to have the other two also. The wealthy tend to have power and prestige. The powerful usually gain prestige and wealth, and the prestigious are likely to be people of

wealth and power. People who have only one of these attributes will seldom be content until they have the other two. In
our society, the usual path to success is first to acquire wealth
and then gradually to gain prestige and power.

Wealth

Who would question that wealth is a major proof of success?
Those who have it are treated with deference and honour,
while those who lack it are usually relegated to social
insignificance and, at times, to disgrace.

Christians in the early church, who should have known
better, often gave preference to the rich and humiliated the
poor. James, in his Epistle, cited such practices and condemned them:

> For if a man comes into your assembly with a gold ring and
> dressed in fine clothes, and there also comes in a poor man in
> dirty clothes, and you pay special attention to the one who is
> wearing the fine clothes, and say, 'You sit here in a good place,'
> and you say to the poor man. 'You stand over there, or sit
> down by my footstool,' have you not made distinctions among
> yourselves, and become judges with evil motives? Listen, my
> beloved brethren: did not God choose the poor of this world to
> be rich in faith and heirs of the kingdom which He promised to
> those who love Him? But you have dishonoured the poor man.
> Is it not the rich who oppress you and personally drag you into
> court? (Jas 2:2–6).

When people fail, they may feel that even God rejects them.
Many have found it difficult to believe they are acceptable to
the Almighty after they have been proven unacceptable by
the success criteria of our culture.

Many people have twisted the Judeo-Christian message to
mean that wealth is evidence of superior spiritual stature.
Some Christians make the amount of money a person possesses a means of judging his relationship with God, pointing

out that when the ancient Jews were right with God, they enjoyed such an abundance of things that their cups were full and overflowing. They say that if we keep the Law of God, particularly his command to tithe one tenth of our income to the work of the church, the Lord will prosper us beyond our imagination. Such claims are made in spite of the fact that there are tens of thousands of people in the Third World nations who love the Lord, obey his Law, faithfully tithe, and yet suffer privation beyond our comprehension. Many Christians subconsciously believe that God must be in league with the rich person.

As a boy I remember attending testimony meetings at our church where Christians told how they were poor and beaten people until they accepted Christ as personal Saviour and Lord. Then they would relate how, as a consequence of their new lives in Christ, they suddenly experienced prosperity. Those testimonies always intrigued me because Jesus taught that following him would cost us everything we possessed, and that in the end we could find ourselves—like the apostle Paul—poor, battered, and imprisoned.

Sermons from the pulpit, articles in magazines, and testimonies of successful Christian businessmen at luncheon meetings, all reinforce the creed that Jesus will prosper us if we just walk in his ways. An exaggerated example of this belief is the American television preacher, Reverend Ike. On more than one occasion he has said: 'God doesn't want anybody to be poor. If you believe in him you will believe in yourself, and if you believe in yourself, you will get rich. I'm rich and that's because I believe in God and I believe in Reverend Ike.'

In our society many people ultimately measure a person's worth by the amount of wealth possessed at death. We may have heard people say about someone who has just died: 'He was born poor with humble parents, but by the time he died he was worth millions.' It is as if that is the best thing that can be said about the person.

We even look for the symbols of wealth at the time of death. This is why we provide such lavish funerals. Even if the person was not rich, we want him to appear so in his final display before friends and relatives.

I heard of a funeral in California where a man requested to be buried seated behind the wheel of a brand-new Cadillac, dressed in a tuxedo, with a two-dollar cigar in his mouth. He left the money to ensure that his wish would be fulfilled, and when he died his plan was carried out. The undertaker brought in a huge crane to manoeuvre the car which served as the coffin for the dead man. As he pulled the handle lowering the corpse and Cadillac into the ground, the crane operator was heard to say, 'Man, that's really living!'

Once my daughter and I were taking the Grayline bus tour of Chicago. As our bus stopped in front of a cinema, our guide pointed to an alley, and in a sober manner told us it was there that John Dillinger, the infamous bank robber, was gunned to death by the FBI. Then he added, 'When John Dillinger died, after robbing more than one million dollars from banks across the Midwest, he had only thirty-two cents left to his name.'

My daughter responded, 'What great timing!'

In her opinion, if you have to die, what better time to go than just when the cash is running out? But people do not generally share that opinion. For many, nothing could be worse than to have the final syllables describing existence be the condemning phrase, 'He died penniless.'

Power

Because we want to determine our own destinies, we resent upheaval from forces beyond our control. We enjoy having people be subservient to us, and deem ourselves powerful if we can direct the actions of others.

As Christians we may say we want power in order to do good for others in Christ's name. We may claim that our sole motivation for seeking power is that we see what needs to be done and want a free hand to do it. On such a noble platform, we seek high offices and important appointments. But such purity of purpose is usually more declaration than reality. All who seek power have covert desires which have to do with the ego gratification that possession of power brings.

I have never held power in any significant way, but I did win a primary election, which made me a candidate for the US Congress. While I lost the general election, the very fact that I had been a candidate for my congressional district gave me a certain amount of influence over some minor politicians who held patronage jobs in our district.

At times people in deep trouble would come to me, after they had been unable to get the local political bureaucracy to respond to their needs. I used to love reaching for the phone, calling the bureaucrat who had been causing the problem, and ordering him to do things right—or else. When the troubled person would look at me with gratitude and admiration, I would try to convince myself that my motives were pure; but down deep inside, I had an inkling that I enjoyed the use of my power too much to consider the act purely altruistic.

In many respects, the feminist challenge to the traditional roles of men and women has turned into a power struggle. Husbands who feel victimised in their everyday jobs are reluctant to lose their authority in the home. They hang onto power tenaciously, using the Bible to legitimate the domination of their wives and children.

On the other hand, there are women who feel no sense of significance because they feel that they are under the control of their husbands. Such women resent having to wash the dishes, clean the toilets, and change the nappies while their husbands sit enthroned in comfort, reading the newspaper. These women claim that because they are being treated as servants, they must rebel.

In labour disputes, the issues often have less to do with money than with labour's resentment of 'management's indiscriminate use of power'. The workers want to determine what can and cannot be done to them by the management. They want to be part of the decision-making process. Employers know that frequently an unhappy employee can be appeased without a raise in salary, as long as he is given an increase in power.

Many a foreman has quit his job in frustration because the unions have curtailed his ability to tell the workers what to do. Without power, there does not seem to be much reason to continue on the job, in spite of an attractive salary.

Even the church cannot escape from petty struggles for power. No one can tell how many churches have disintegrated into power struggles, splitting congregations or causing systemic groups to pull out of the church. The spokesmen for the warring camps usually cloak their actions in such idealistic claims as 'standing for truth' or 'being faithful to the gospel'. But we are all too aware that behind such conflicts are people vying for power.

Even as we seek power, we sense something inherently wrong with what we are doing. We are confronted by our Lord Jesus Christ who stands in opposition to our power plays.

During Jesus' temptation (Mt 4), Satan tried to lure him into utilising power in ways that would compel people to grant him allegiance by:

● feeding them bread made from stones,

● astounding them as he floated down from the Temple pinnacle and landed unhurt,

● establishing earthly authority over the systems and peoples of the world.

But Jesus refused to use power to win followers. Instead, he emptied himself of power and chose to win us from a position of weakness—the cross. The Scripture says that he became an obedient Servant, obedient unto death, 'even death on a cross' (Phil 2:8). He was born in weakness and he died in weakness; for through that weakness, the Father worked his will in history, as salvation became a reality. Christ wants us to give up our power plays and attempts to dominate others, and to follow him into servanthood.

A world that worships power, and sees it as an ultimate mark of success, has a hard time comprehending a kind of success that is based on the mutual submission of love. Friedrich Nietzsche, the atheistic, existentialist philosopher, claimed that the 'will to power' was the most basic drive of the human personality, motivating all of human behaviour. I believe there is more to Nietzsche's claim than we want to admit. Power *is* a mark of success within our society, and the human appetite for it seems insatiable.

Prestige

If we lack money and power, we can still feel successful if we have the respect of our peers. As a young minister without wealth or power, I loved to be called 'Reverend'. It was an ego trip for me when I was asked to pray at important public gatherings; I thrilled at the honour of addressing prestigious meetings. When I was asked to fly from Pennsylvania to speak at a convention on the West Coast, that seemed proof that I was somebody special. I might be short on power and low on cash, but I felt as successful as any millionaire or congressman when I just 'humbly' preached the gospel to a few thousand people.

Employers joke about the fact that if they can't give employees a raise in salary, they can satisfy them with more prestigious titles. At social gatherings, we love to impress people by convincing them that we hold important positions. We feel successful if people are impressed upon hearing our answer to the question, 'What do you do?'

We all play for prestige. Public figures long to see their names in the New Year's Honours List. Schoolboys pay a high price to be known as part of the school football team. Young girls fantasise over the status they will enjoy when the gang at school knows whom they are dating. We all tend to play oneupmanship with each other, and at the same time claim to be followers of Jesus who 'made himself of no reputation (Phil 2:7, KJV).

Feeling successful by means of prestige is a complex problem for women. Traditionally, they obtained their prestige vicariously, by borrowing it from their husbands. If their husbands had jobs that brought positive recognition, the women felt that they too were important. However, the feminist movement is changing all of that, saying each woman should have her own accomplishments to earn the respect of others.

For many a woman, this call to individual success has come too late. She has been comfortable in sharing her husband's successes, content to smile benevolently as he receives honours at the Rotary Club's Ladies Night and graciously tells the crowd, 'I would not be here today if it weren't for my dear wife who has stood by me through thick and thin, and supported me in all my endeavours.'

It seems like a dirty trick to play on such women. After becoming used to feeling successful because they are married to successful husbands, they are now told that it won't do any more. They are informed that this age requires each woman to earn status through her own achievements. Such a challenge can create insecurities, particularly for women over forty years of age.

When I evaluate my own attitudes, I find that the only time I am seriously tempted to lie is when it will enhance my personal status. I have a tendency to make myself out as more than I really am, to paint myself bigger than life. I exaggerate my successes, minimise my failures, and offer myself to the world as somebody who has done great things. Oh, what a sorry contrast I make to Jesus who was willing to make himself nothing for our sakes! God honours the humility of his Son by giving him 'the name which is above every name, that at the name of Jesus every knee should bow... and every tongue confess that Jesus Christ is Lord' (Phil 2:9–10).

Those who seek prestige will never get it from God; but those who are willing to be humble and take 'the inferior seats at the banquet' will find that the heavenly Father calls them to the places of honour which they know they do not deserve (see Luke 14:7–11). The Scripture warns that those who seek the praise of the world have their reward here on earth, but those who are willing to serve in secret, without any thought of public recognition, will find themselves honoured in heaven (Mt 6:1–6).

Christians and the big three

Because the world sees wealth, power, and prestige as the indicators of success, we have been conditioned to seek them with all of our might. But our Lord has different criteria for evaluating success. He calls us away from society's symbols of success and urges us to seek after 'His kingdom and His righteousness' (Mt 6:33). Many who are considered least important by society may find themselves sitting in places of honour at the great banquet feast in the world to come.

Wealth, power, and prestige can corrupt those who possess them. *Wealth* can delude us into a kind of self-sufficiency and denial of our need of God. It is easy to become so over-protective of our economic interests that we oppose compassionate social policies which would diminish our wealth.

Power can turn us into megalomaniacs. Desire to dominate others can lead us to diminish their humanity, as well as our own. Sometimes we sacrifice those who are nearest to us in order to achieve power.

Cravings for *prestige* can lead us into destructive pride and egotism that know no bounds, until our need for the world to focus on us becomes obnoxious.

Yet we must remember that wealth, power, and prestige have great potential for good. It is only their wrong use which is evil. Our Lord owns the cattle on a thousand hills and the wealth in every mine. He has the power to hold the universe together or to destroy it in an instant. But he uses his wealth, power, and prestige to express love and to benefit everyone.

If we wish to be governed by God's will, we can learn to use our wealth, power, and prestige for others, and to extend the kingdom of God in the world.

2

Successful People Can Be Disciples

It is not necessary to be a failure in order to be a follower of Jesus. Successful people are also called to follow after the Master. The Scripture teaches that those holding trophies of success must be willing to lay them at the foot of the cross, willingly surrendering their wealth, power, and prestige to Jesus. It is a beautiful thing to see people who are willing to use the success they have earned in obedience to the will of God.

Do you feel like a failure?

There are not many people who truly feel successful. One of the great ironies in this world is that those who achieve great success in the eyes of others often feel like failures themselves. We all know people who seem driven to achieve more and more to convince themselves that they are successful. In a sense that was the basic problem of President Nixon. Regardless of what others may say, I believe he was basically a good man. His downfall resulted from the fact that he never felt himself to be completely successful, no matter what he achieved.

It was this that led to Watergate. For Nixon it was not enough to be a successful candidate; he craved a total victory that would be a complete mandate to power. He wanted election results that would declare him so popular that his cravings for self-affirmation would be satisfied. But in the end, this desire for affirmation drove him to self-destruction.

The significant other

What is it that gives us a sense of satisfaction about our successes? What is it that makes some people feel successful—in spite of the fact that the world in general declares them to be failures, while others have a sense of failure—in spite of the fact that the world thinks them successful? The answers to these questions lie in one important truth: *we are successful if the most significant people in our lives deem us successful.*

Perhaps we all know a man who has accomplished great things but lacks any sense of self-fulfilment because he has not achieved success in the eyes of his father. If that father is the *significant other* in his life, the applause of thousands will not mean as much to him as the recognition that could be given by that one person, his own father.

I know a woman who is a fantastic pianist and widely known as an accomplished artist. Nevertheless, she feels a deep sense of failure because her father, also a famous pianist, has never given her the approval she desperately craves. She works incessantly and suffers constantly, striving to gain success in his eyes. Wealth, power, and prestige mean nothing without the approval of the ones we love.

The lover knows that success means being viewed as successful in the eyes of a significant other. I remember the lyrics of a song from my teenage years that went like this:

> If they made me a king, I'd still be a slave to you.
> If I had everything, I'd still be a knave to you.
> If I ruled the earth, what would life be worth,
> If I hadn't the right to you?

Progressive significant others

At different stages of our lives, the significant others change. Those persons whose approval gives us the inner feeling of success are not the same throughout the life cycle. Children will puff up with pleasure when they do something that makes 'Mummy and Daddy' proud of them. Nothing destroys them more or leaves them with a greater sense of failure than an awareness that their parents disapprove of what they have done. As a boy, I remember rushing home with a good school report to be praised by my mother and father. If they said that I was a good boy because I had done well, I knew that there was nothing more to be achieved. My life revolved around this parental approval.

For teenagers, the significant others tend to be in their peer groups. Most of us can recall periods in our lives when the approval of 'the gang' supplanted the opinions of parents. We may even have developed an indifference to parental approval and looked with disdain on those school classmates who were still primarily motivated by a desire to please their parents.

Our male chauvinistic society has been particularly hard on boys who work overtime to gain the praise of their mothers. They have been called 'Mummy's boys' and regarded as far less 'macho' than most boys imagine themselves to be.

The years of passage into adulthood are years when the significant others are young people of their own age group. If *they* think a person is 'cool', then he is bathed in the ecstasy of feeling successful. And then, too, the disapproval of parents can easily be endured.

As I think back to my own teen years, I know that of all the members of the peer group who gave me a sense of significance, none were more important than those of the opposite sex. Girls who were popular with the boys felt like successful 'somebodies'. Nothing diminished a girl's sense of worth more than to lack a high rating with the boys at school.

Among the boys there was a willingness to do anything to

earn the admiration of special girls. I remember trying to get selected for every team, hoping that my athletic prowess would make the girls I liked worship me. I fantasised constantly about scoring the winning touchdown, dropping the winning basket through the hoop just as the gun went off in the tournament game, or winning the cross-country championship with a sudden burst of speed, overtaking my opponents just before the finish line. For me the games were only a means to an end—and that end was to win more approval and admiration from the girls than any of the other guys. Success meant gaining the approval of my peers, particularly my female peers.

The generalised other

When trying to define the significant others for adults, we have a more complicated task. We are not quite sure whose approval adults try to gain. It is too simple to say that, like teenagers, they want to impress their peers. Adults want more than that. They want approval from the world in general. They want people whom they have never met to know of them and admire them. Adults wish to enjoy wide recognition and universally recognized symbols of success.

George Herbert Mead, a prominent, early twentieth-century sociologist, used the expression *the generalised other* to denote that amorphous group towards which adults orient their behaviour. How often do we act in a particular manner in order that 'they' might approve of us? When we think of failure, we fear that 'they' will despise us. It is before this nonspecific jury that we plead our case for personal worth. It is the verdict we think 'they' pass on us that holds the basis for our well-being.

But who are *they*—these persons who hold our sense of self-worth so carelessly in their hands? *They* are everybody, and yet *they* are nobody special. *They* are people we have never met, but who may prove to be the most important persons in our lives. Those whom Mead called the *generalised other*, Nietzsche called the *herd* and the Bible calls the *world*. For adults, the generalised other becomes the significant other whose praise gives feelings of success.

Competition and fear of failure

We respect success more when it is competitively achieved. Those who inherit wealth, power, and prestige are not looked upon as genuinely successful. Somehow they seem to lack the virtues of truly successful people who have earned these things on their own.

In this competitive struggle, which all of us seem compelled to enter, there is the constant fear of failure. And it is this fear of failing which elicits some of our most pathetic behaviour. The child, afraid that he has not done enough to earn the approval of his parents, will boast of achievements that were never his, or exaggerate what he has accomplished. The teenager, aware that acceptance by his peers must be carefully engineered by imitating their lifestyles, lives in fear that he might do, say or even think something that would leave him alienated and alone. The adult who isn't quite sure whom he is trying to please has fears that turn into diffused anxiety, leaving him immobilised and incapable of taking the risks necessary for a fulfilled and successful life.

Another option

Christianity provides an alternative to the threats of failure that loom so large in our success-hungry society. There is deliverance from the fears that sap the joy from living. The gospel is the good news that there is another option which keeps the success game from being the only game in town.

When we become Christians, we invite Jesus to be the Significant Other in our lives. We allow him to displace the generalised other, in the language of Mead; or the world, in the language of the Scriptures. To be *Christian* means that we seek his approval and learn to count what the world says about us as secondary. It is difficult to please both Jesus and the generalised other at the same time. As Christians, our ultimate calling is to do 'that which is pleasing in His sight' (Heb 13:21).

When we orient ourselves to Jesus, seeking to gain his approval, we will discover that we are accepted just as we are. Jesus does not require some great achievement before he affirms our worth. To each of us he says, 'If you had been the only person who ever lived in time and history, you are so precious to me that I would have died to save only you.'

We don't have to work to gain positions of privilege at his right hand, for he has already declared us to be heirs of God and joint heirs with him. This means that ultimately the wealth of the universe is ours. It means we have been assigned a status higher than the angels. It means we receive power to join the family of God, and to serve man and God according to his will.

It is difficult for us to believe these truths because of the idea that success is competitively earned. We find it hard to be the heirs of spiritual wealth, power, and prestige. We want to do something wonderful for God, to be deserving of these things.

Paul tried to convince the early Christians that 'by grace you have been saved through faith; and that not of yourselves, it is the gift of God; not as a result of works, that no one should boast (Eph 2:8–9). We go through life tortured by the belief that we have not done enough to be worthy of his approval, in spite of the fact that he tells us we are approved by him because of what his Son has done on our behalf. Nothing can take his loving approval away from us. 'Neither death, nor life, nor angels, nor principalities, nor things present, nor things to come, nor powers, nor height, nor depth, nor any other created thing, shall be able to separate us from the love of God, which is in Christ Jesus our Lord (Rom 8:38–39).

This is the meaning of grace—approval and loving acceptance by God without having to achieve anything. It is that inner feeling of success which comes from being accepted, appreciated, and wanted by the ultimate Significant Other. For the child the word is: 'When your mother and father forsake you then the Lord will take you up.' For the teenager, the good news is that Jesus is: 'The Friend ... closer than a brother.' For the adult there is the question: 'If Christ be for you, who can be against you?' (See Psalm 27:10; Proverbs 18:24; Romans 8:31.)

3
Successes and Sufferings of Little People

Young children generally feel successful when they sense that they have earned the approval of their parents. Sigmund Freud narrowed that to mean that children feel the most successful when they gain approval from the parent of the opposite sex. He believed that in early childhood, boys strive primarily to earn the affection and the approval of their mothers, while girls want these from their fathers.

Freud called this tendency in boys the Oedipus complex and in girls the Electra complex. Boys up to about seven to ten years of age will feel successful if they know that their mothers are proud of them. Girls in this period of development will feel successful if they know that their fathers consider them special and beautiful people.

We are aware of the limitations in much of what Freud taught, particularly his disregard of spiritual dimensions to personality. Nevertheless, his understanding of the relationships that exist between children and parents should not be overlooked; he offered valuable insights into human behaviour.

Parent approval is essential

As a boy I loved to hear my mother say to me, 'I'm proud of you.' Once, when I was seven, I had a special part in a short

27

play put on by our class. I remember how important it was for me that my mother come to see the play and how proud I felt when she hugged me after it was over and told me that I had done so well. The achievements of Alexander the Great could not have made him feel more successful than I felt that Friday afternoon in the school. My childhood fantasies usually revolved around doing something so wonderful that I could convince my mother that she had the best and most heroic boy in the whole world.

At school or church I loved it when I had the opportunity to make things that I could take home and show her. I cannot tell you how happy I was when, after bringing home a letter holder made out of lollipop sticks, my mother asked with apparent wonder, 'Did you make this? You didn't really make this, did you?'

I remember jumping up and down with excitement and saying, 'Yes I did; yes I did! I made that and I made it for you, Mum. I made it for you.' The feeling was so good that I wanted to go back and make more and better things. The feeling of success which pervaded my little body came from doing the things that gained her approval.

The Oedipus complex in boys is paralleled in girls by the Electra complex. This simply means that little girls get emotionally 'hung up' on their fathers. I have interviewed many women, asking them to reflect on what made them feel successful in their early years. Each of them conveyed how important her father was in making her feel successful. One woman told me about the happiest moment in her life. As a seven-year-old girl, she played in a recital at her piano teacher's studio and her father was there proudly smiling.

Other women told about dressing up and trying to look pretty for their fathers, and how pleased they felt when their fathers paid attention to the way they looked. Each of these women had a deep childhood longing to be 'Daddy's little girl'. They wanted their fathers to feel proud to have such talented and attractive daughters

Parent approval withheld

In many cases the parents' unwillingness to give sought-for approval has had lasting and detrimental consequences in a child's future development. A friend of mine researched the lives of famous people who were noted for outstanding accomplishments. His study showed that many of them became overachievers because of the kinds of relationships they had had with parents in their earliest years.

As a case in point, imagine a little boy who strives very hard to earn his mother's approval but never feels he gains it. He works harder and harder, always hoping that if he accomplishes more she will give him what he desperately wants. She withholds approval and so he goes on pressing for higher and higher levels of achievement, hoping to win the praise of this woman who subconsciously looms as the significant other in his life.

Some boys never outgrow their felt need for the approval of their mothers. Unless children receive parental approval in the preadolescent period, they find it difficult to allow others to take the place of parents as their significant others. They become, as psychologists say, fixated in a childlike state. Throughout their lives they function as little children, ever hoping that their accomplishments will be admired by their parents.

Some parents think it is an act of love *not* to give easy approval to their children for the accomplishments. They think that by not showing early satisfaction with what their children accomplish, they will encourage them to do better. When their children proudly come home with school reports showing all *A*'s except for a *B* in one subject, instead of getting applause from their parents, they are confronted with, 'How come you got a *B*?'

While this tactic may motivate children to work harder in school for higher grades, it can also push them towards becoming incessant workers who are never satisfied, no matter what they achieve, and who never feel successful, no

matter what other people say. My friend who researched
famous people found that very few of them had a sense of satisfaction about life or any feeling of joy about what they had
done. As great as their accomplishments were, these people
lived with childhood impressions that they still could do better.

Encourage your children

In opposition to these childrearing practices, the apostle Paul
teaches us: 'Fathers, do not exasperate your children; instead,
bring them up in the training and instruction of the Lord'
(Eph 6:4, NIV).

Parents need this biblical admonition to keep them from
pushing their children too hard and distorting their personalities. It's all right to urge children towards accomplishment,
but it needs to be done in grace rather than by withholding
approval and encouragement.

The way God relates to his children is the best model for
encouraging children to higher levels of achievement, without inflicting emotional hurt.

1. *He forgives*. As he shows us how to handle our own failures, we can learn from him how to deal with the failures and
accomplishments of our children. When we fail the Lord, he
not only *forgives us*, but also *justifies us*. Though it may seem
childlike, I still choose to describe justification as it was
explained to me when I was a boy—God treating me 'just-as-
if-I-never-sinned'. That simple statement is a truthful por-
trayal of the way God handles our sins and failures: they are
buried in the deepest sea and remembered no more (see
Micah 7:19). We are told, 'There is therefore now no condem-
nation for those who are in Christ Jesus' (Rom 8:1). Our failures are never held against us once we have confessed them
and asked for forgiveness. Parents should do the same when
their children fail, by helping them to admit their failures, to
learn from them, and then to leave them forgotten, where
they can no longer cause depression.

Jesus not only forgets our failures, but also praises us for the good things that we do. We are told by him that even a glass of cool water given in his name shall have its reward (see Matthew 10:42). In the biblical description of Judgement Day, he remembers good things we have done even after we have forgotten, recalling that we fed the hungry, clothed the naked, and visited the sick and the captives in prison. When he reminds his people of their forgotten good deeds, they are surprised and ask, 'When did we see You hungry and feed You, naked and clothe You, sick and imprisoned and visit You?'

Then Jesus will say, 'Inasmuch as you have done it unto the least of these My brethren, you have done it unto Me' (see Matthew 25:34–40).

What a Saviour! He forgets our failures, but remembers every good thing that we do and rewards us now and for ever for our limited accomplishments. This is a true model of childrearing for parents everywhere!

2. *He motivates.* Jesus motivates his people to higher levels of achievement, not by withholding his symbols of love and approval, but by trying to develop a love within us that will result in service for his kingdom. He does not try to motivate us to do the good things by promising us his love and acceptance. Instead, he surrounds us with love and acceptance, hoping that out of gratitude we will be prodded to do more and more for him and for others. The joy that comes from growing awareness that we *are* his and are of infinite worth, and that even our simplest good deeds have significance, motivates us to give more of ourselves for what will please him.

As Jesus has treated us, so we should treat our children. We must accept them even when they do things which we believe to be unacceptable. When they fail we must call them to repentance but at the same time communicate to them that when they are forgiven, their failures are forgotten and not held against them. We must exalt their accomplishments and show our pride in even the little things they do for us.

Children's reactions to unwise parents

1. *Love-Hate*. Parents who do not learn from Jesus to deal with their children in grace may create ambivalent feelings. On the one hand, their children may love them because it is the nature of most children to love their parents. But on the other hand, that love may be mixed with intense hatred and resentment for parents who make life seem impossible.

Children may also hate their parents for the feelings of inadequacy the parents have caused them to feel. This is particularly evident when parents constantly tell children that they could be doing better. This leaves the children confused about their own emotions and with ambivalent feelings towards their parents. It is enough to turn some children into neurotics.

2. *Despair*. Another reaction to parents who withhold enthusiastic approval of their children, regardless of their achievements, is for the children to simply give up trying to please them. Interviews with children, particularly teenagers, reveal that they often despair of ever earning praise from their parents. I remember one boy saying to me sadly, 'What's the use? No matter what I do, it is never enough to please my mum and dad. I do my very best, but is that OK with them? No way! So you know what? I don't care anymore.'

3. *Delinquency*. Sometimes resentment against overly demanding parents will result in what many social scientists call a *reaction formation*. This means that the child will do just the opposite of what the parents desire. Much delinquent behaviour is the working out of resentment that children feel as a consequence of their love-hate relationship with their parents. They use delinquent acts to retaliate for their parents' failure to give them sufficient praise. The irony of this state of affairs is that very often the parents show more love and acceptance towards their children when they are delinquent than they showed when their children were trying to do what was good and right.

A typical case study of such a child might reveal a girl who tries to look pretty, do well in school, and be proper in her conduct, hoping to gain the adoration of her father. When he fails to appreciate her, she decides to punish him. The easiest way to do that is to become just the opposite of what he wants her to be. As she moves into her teenage years, she gives up studying, becomes sexually promiscuous, and goes out of her way to flaunt her improprieties before her father. When he tries to tell her how much she is hurting him, she subconsciously says to herself, 'Good!'

The father tries to reach out to her with all kinds of expressions of affirmation and love, hoping that he can influence her for good. If only he had offered her these emotional gifts earlier, she might not ever have behaved as she did.

The apostle Paul wrote to fathers: 'Do not exasperate your children, that they may not lose heart' (Col 3:21).

The relationships that children have with their parents dramatically colour the ways these children will be able to think about God. Many social scientists argue that what children believe, think, and feel about their heavenly Father will be highly influenced by what they think about their earthly fathers. If their earthly parents seem unaccepting and disapproving, regardless of achievement, the children will come to regard their heavenly Father as unaccepting and disapproving.

Pastors often tell me how they struggle with people who seem incapable of believing that God loves and accepts them or sees infinite worth in them. These people have been conditioned, through early childhood experiences with their own parents to view their heavenly Father as ungracious. Their pastors experience the frustration of being unable to lead them towards knowing their worth in God's sight, even after showing them verse after verse from the Scriptures about God's love and acceptance.

When I see how early childhood experiences can condition persons so that their images of God are mainly negative, I realise the miraculous nature of conversion. Only the Holy

Spirit can undo emotional damage from early childhood experiences. Only a miracle can change the negative attitudes towards God generated by the bad relationships children have had with their parents.

The miracle of being born again

For several years I lectured at an Ivy League university. One of my postgraduate students inadvertently spoke a truth which he himself did not comprehend: 'Doctor, there is no way to undo damage done by faulty social conditioning in the early stages of childhood. The hurt created by parents can never be overcome. The only hope would be if the individual would be able to go back and start over again. If somehow the individual could be born again.'

I responded by saying, 'But that's the good news. Each of us can be born again.' The Holy Spirit working in our lives can enable us to overcome what has been and to become what was otherwise impossible. Basic attitudinal structures can miraculously be broken down and new ones constructed. Deeply established negative images of the nature of God can be erased and new ones drawn in their place. The Scriptures teach: 'If any man is in Christ, he is a new creature: the old things passed away; behold, new things have come' (2 Cor 5:17).

I cannot explain the ways in which this miracle occurs. I cannot describe the work of the Holy Spirit. But I can tell you that I have seen the impossible happen. I have seen personality structures altered and new orientations and attitudes towards God come into being.

I cannot explain the process, but I can point to the change that takes place when a person asks the resurrected Jesus, whom Christians claim is ever present, to take possession of him, to invade his personality, to enter his psyche. Some of my fellow social scientists chide my convictions on these matters, calling them expressions of mysticism. It may be true that I am somewhat mystical; but to the scientifically minded,

I can say that the results of surrendering to Jesus are empirically verifiable.

Children want to please their parents

The tendency for children to work intensely to please their parents can easily be exploited. I have to wonder how many children have been baptised or confirmed into the membership of the church because of a deep desire to please their parents. I know that when I was a pastor there were many children who came to me asking for baptism primarily for this reason. I am convinced that many people have become missionaries or pastors for wrong reasons. In early childhood they learned that if they went into these church vocations, their parents would be very proud.

During the time I was host of a talk show on a Philadelphia television station, my fifteen-year-old son was a guest on my show. One day I asked him if he felt I had ever pressured him in the selection of a life's vocation. He replied, 'Not directly. No matter what I mention as a possible career you say, "OK, that's nice." But if I say I'm thinking of becoming a minister, you light up and go bananas.'

I hope and pray that if my son ever decides to be a minister, his motivation will be something other than a desire to gain my approval.

Since children are anxious to please, parents must be very careful of this kind of manipulation. When children do right things for wrong reasons, they may suffer confusion and resentment when they are grown-up. As young adults develop the capacity to reflect upon the motivations behind their youthful decisions, they sometimes deliberately reverse those decisions. For instance, if they realise that their basic reason for choosing to be baptised or joining the church was because of manipulation by their parents, they may become resentful and reject Christianity altogether.

These grown-up children may not only reject the God that

their parents manipulated them into accepting, but also the manipulators themselves. They may become angry with their parents and estranged from them when the children realise that their own desire to please was exploited unfairly.

On the other hand, we must admit that there are more people whose desire to please their parents led them to seriously consider Christ and accept him as Saviour, without negative effects. When children sense that Jesus is important to their parents, they may become genuinely open to the gospel in a rich and meaningful way.

Parents need to communicate to their children that they are accepted and loved whether they accept Christ as a personal Saviour or not. Acceptance of Christ should not be a condition for gaining parental approval.

Comparison can be abusive

One of the worst abuses by parents is trying to elicit great accomplishments from children by comparing them with their brothers and sisters or with children from outside the family. The mother who says, 'Why can't you be like your sister?' may be responsible for setting brother and sister against each other in such a way that they can never enjoy one another. Such children may never feel successful unless they are outdoing their brothers and sisters. How sad it is to see parents stimulate rivalry between their own children so that family solidarity is lost, love is diminished, and even hatred comes into play.

Parents should be committed to making each child feel that he or she is appreciated in a special way. Parents should be affirming the uniqueness of each child rather than exploiting comparisons. To be a truly Christian parent is to be sensitive to those traits which make each child special, and to show appreciation for that uniqueness.

4
School Daze

When children enter school, important transitions occur in their lives. One of the most important is when the children begin to regard the recognition granted by teachers to be as important as that granted by parents. Whereas being successful formerly meant approval from parents, children in school begin to treat approval from their teachers with equal importance. To many children teachers become glorious, all-knowing, all-powerful creatures. Receiving positive feedback from these teachers affirms the children in almost miraculous ways. Likewise, some children who feel put down or unappreciated by their teachers develop very poor self-images which may result in inferiority complexes that torture them for the rest of their lives.

My wife has told me many times about the influence her teacher had on her when she was twelve. He was handsome, intelligent, kind, and seemed almost godlike. Pleasing him became the primary motivation of her life. She did her homework with great dedication and was thrilled every time a paper was returned with an *A* on it. Having the teacher praise her work gave her a sense of success about life that no one could challenge.

I remember the teacher I had when I was ten. She loved me and delighted in my accomplishments. This made me want to do more and more good work for her. I wished this wonderful lady were my age so that we could grow up together and be married. Nothing could have seemed better than to spend the rest of my life with this most significant person. For me there was no question but that success lay in doing things she thought were worthwhile, and doing them in a way that she would applaud.

Why was she so special? She was the first teacher who made me feel that she really believed in me, and so helped me to believe in myself. She was the first one who saw me as a success in academic work. I wonder if I would be a college lecturer today if Miss Barr had not shown me the success I could feel through academic accomplishments.

Teachers as significant others

Any parent knows how important teachers are to children. What teachers say often is more important than what parents say. Teachers can become the ultimate source of truth. I remember when arguments with my daughter would conclude with her haughty assertion that I was wrong because what I said differed with what her teacher had said. When the words 'My teacher told me' prefaced her statements, I knew their was no point in disputing them. The teacher had replaced me as the significant other in her life.

One of the amusing events in rearing my daughter was the time when she discovered that one of her teachers had been a postgraduate student of mine. The idea that her father could be her teacher's teacher was hard for her to handle, and I know that I went up in her estimation because her teacher respected my opinions.

Lack of recognition

The role of the teacher as the significant other for the growing child has potential for both good and evil. We have cited ways in which children can become more successful pupils if they have teachers who believe in them and praise their accomplishments. However, there are cases in which teachers have failed their students by withholding appreciation and praise when children have made efforts to earn these responses. After my daughter had turned in a science project on which she had spent many hours, she told me in a discouraged manner, 'You know, it really didn't make any difference at all that I did that work. The teacher didn't think what I made was special at all.'

A friend of mine is an angry leader in the Chicano communities of the American Southwest. His most intense anger is over what he says the Anglo schoolteachers are doing to Latino children. He tells me that many of the teachers do not expect Mexican-American children to accomplish much, and consequently, they don't. These teachers do not give recognition to the efforts made by Chicano children when they try to learn, and the children come away from their classes with no sense of accomplishment. My friend claims that if these children are to feel successful, they must have teachers who believe in them and expect them to learn. If the children cannot be made to feel successful in school, they will want to drop out to get away from those who foster their feelings of insignificance.

As a sociologist, I am convinced that feeling like a failure at school is a major cause of juvenile delinquency. Children retreat from classrooms and from teachers who make them feel unsuccessful, and look for some other group that will give them more positive feelings. The youngster who is willing to do something daringly antisocial can gain instantaneous praise from the gang that hangs out on the street corner. If being foulmouthed, tough, and defiant are traits which the gang will praise, children craving for approval will quickly acquire them.

A child's self-image

Parents need to be very concerned about the effects that teachers are having on their children. Parents cannot assume that school experiences are going well simply because children are getting good marks and seem to be mastering their academic assignments. School is much more than reading, writing, and arithmetic. Perhaps the most important thing that any child can receive from the years spent in school is a positive self-image that leaves him convinced of his personal worth.

Parents should not be deterred from interfering in any teacher-child relationship that seems to be having a detrimental effect on the child. Children are far too precious for their self-images to be distorted. If little can be done to alter the negative effects that a teacher is having on a child, then the parents should consider having that child removed to another class where the effects of teacher-child interaction will be more positive. If need be, the child may have to move to a different school.

Too often, parents think that it is best not to interfere in school situations, even when they are alarmed by what is happening to their child. They have heard other parents suggest that it is good for the child to struggle through a negative teacher-child arrangement, even if it leaves the child depressed about himself and antagonistic about school. Nothing could be further from the truth.

Parents and children who have the right to expect the school to provide teachers who affirm pupils, enable them to believe in themselves, and give them feelings of positive achievement. When this right is denied, the parents must see the head teacher or school counsellor in order to change the situation. If they allow the child to try to resolve such a problem for himself, it could be too much for him to handle, and the influence of the teacher too great for the child to overcome.

Usually the other members of the child's class will come to

view him through the teacher's eyes. The opinion of the teacher is so highly respected by most pupils that when the teacher defines a child as a failure in some way, the other pupils in the class reinforce that judgement, and provide such a negative social environment for the child that coping becomes impossible.

How are your children taught?

In analysing how school experiences influence children to feel like successes or failures, we must pay attention not only to the role of teachers, but also to the very processes by which education is carried out.

Marshall McLuhan has said, 'The medium is the message.' The *way* children are taught communicates messages of far greater importance than *what* they are taught. Let me illustrate what I mean.

When I was ten years old, I regularly walked to school with my good friend Albert, who was the smartest boy in the class. One particular day Albert and I walked to school together, went into our classroom and took our seats as usual. The teacher started class by giving us good news. 'Today we're going to play a game.'

I was thrilled. I hated school and loved games. The idea of playing instead of studying made me happy.

She said, 'Boys and girls, we're going to play baseball.' This was almost too much. I loved baseball. Then she said, 'We're going to play spelling baseball.'

The second announcement deflated me. I hated spelling. As the child of an Italian immigrant family, I found spelling impossible, and not because I was stupid. Any language that spells pneumonia with a 'p' has to be devoid of rationality.

The teacher chose captains for the two teams. Naturally, Albert was chosen. The other team captain was a girl named Mary. I couldn't stand Mary; she was one of those perfect children who did everything just right. She dressed right, she spoke right, she walked right, and she smiled right. She was constantly held up before us as a shining example of what we were supposed to be. I don't know how many times children in our class were put down with the statement, 'Why can't you be good like Mary?'

The captains were allowed to pick their team members. I sat there feeling 'cool' because Albert was my friend and I assumed that he would pick me first. I was wrong; Albert did not pick me first. He did not pick me second. He did not pick me third. I began to wave my hand in his face in the frantic style that is characteristic of young children who want to be chosen. Still Albert did not choose me. He seemed to look right through me and went on selecting other children.

I was shaken but I *was* learning. What I was learning was that in this game, friendship did not count. The only thing that counted was how successfully a child could spell. It was then and there that I learned that, within this competitive system, success was more important than friendship. Acceptance and rejection depended upon success, and success alone.

The teacher didn't understand when three weeks later she caught me cheating in a spelling test. She said to me, 'Tony, don't you know you can't learn how to spell by copying the answers off someone else's paper?' Foolish teacher! Didn't she know that I didn't care about spelling? All I cared about was the evidence of success that would earn me the acceptance of my peers.

The selection of team members continued and still I was left behind. Albert had forsaken me. Finally, there were only two of us not chosen – just me and another kid who went to a special school the next year. Even then, Albert didn't want me. But I was assigned to his team.

As I stood glued against the wall of the classroom staring at the opposing team, I waited nervously for my turn, dreading it as it drew near. I failed on the first word I was asked to spell, *grasshopper*. I didn't know the word had two *Ps*. The teacher's words were painful to hear: 'You're out. Now take your seat.'

No one in the world can feel more alone than the first one out in spelling baseball. As I crawled to my seat, all the members of my team booed me, and to make my humiliation complete, the members of the opposing team cheered my failure. As I tried to disappear under my desk by slumping as low as possible, my only hope was that others would fail too; then I would not be the only one out. People who fail always feel like that. Failure is a little less tortuous if there are others who share it with you.

The teacher turned to the other team and asked 'Does anyone here know how to spell *grasshopper*?'

Little Mary knew. I can still see and hear her. 'Grasshopper,' she said (in such a prissy manner). 'G-R-A-S-S-H-O-P-P-E-R.' With each letter she swung her shoulders, and as each letter sounded, it was like a knife being stabbed into my stomach. I felt like I was dying.

My failure means your success

I was learning a lesson that had nothing to do with spelling. The lesson was this: Mary's success was built on my failure; my failure was a condition for Mary's triumph. This is the lesson that prepares the individual to live in our kind of world. Businessmen who have learned it well can delight in the failure of their competitors, knowing that those failures are their own opportunities to succeed. Some people may even long for the failures of their closest friends.

This is one place where a dominant Western value runs contrary to the values inherent in Scripture. The apostle Paul warns us against such feelings when he tells us in 1 Corinthians 13 that the loving Christian rejoices not in the failures but in the successes of others.

It is a cop-out to shrug our shoulders and say, 'That's the system. You've got to learn to live with it.' We *don't* have to.

Existentialist Jean Paul Sartre spoke against this human

tendency to accept the structures of society as though they were invulnerable to change. He called this 'bad faith'.

God wants us to struggle against 'the principalities and powers' that lessen our humanity. I believe this means that when a social practice diminishes an individual's self-worth, that practice must be challenged by the people of God.

I am convinced that most children who hate school feel that way because the educational system makes them feel like failures. Most children love discovering and exploring what is new, and they are thrilled when their perception of the world is expanded. Learning new things makes them feel wonderfully grown-up.

Very often parents will say to me, 'I know my child is intelligent. He has a good head on his shoulders, but he doesn't want to work. He just won't do his homework. I know that he could do well in school if he would just try. Tell me, Dr Campolo, why doesn't he want to study?'

Take a good look at the system. Your child may be refusing to study because he doesn't want to be part of a system that refuses to affirm him as a person or give him positive feelings of self-worth. His only way of rebelling against the system is non-co-operation. For many children school is agony.

Grandiose dreams

Some children cope with their present feelings of failure by convincing themselves that they will someday be famous and achieve such great things, that they will be admired far and wide, particularly by those who scorn them in the present. Unfortunately, their dreams are usually grandiose beyond any possibility of coming true. Most of these children will always feel like failures.

The Bible teaches us that 'young men shall see visions' and 'old men shall dream dreams' (Acts 2:17). When this is not the case, the Scriptures tell us that the people perish (see Proverbs 29:18). Christians should challenge an educational system that so fills children with a sense of failure that they escape into an unrealistic world of fantasies.

One of the saddest discussions I've ever had was with a four-teen-year-old black student who had been raised in the ghetto and denied a valid education. He could hardly read by the time he was eight. His teacher viewed him as hopeless and his class-mates considered him stupid. Nevertheless, when I spoke with him, he told me that when he grew up he was going to be the 'best and most famous brain surgeon in the world'.

I don't think that it is racist to suggest that this youngster had unrealistic dreams. I understood why he had them. He seemed to be saying to me, and to himself, 'Someday I'll show them! They might laugh at me now, but someday I'll be so famous that they will be proud to have known me!'

No matter what this young man achieves in life, I think he will feel like a failure. He will experience the frustration that comes to a person who lacks the means to realise his goals. As his hurt turns to anger, who knows how much he will try to get back at a world that has caused him so much pain?

Christian schools?

When we consider what the normative educational process does to children in the state school system, we are prone to ask whether it might not be better to have children educated in Christian schools. Over the past decade, many such insti-tutions have sprung up, offering us an alternative to the secu-lar educational system which communicates the dominant values of the culture rather than the values inherent in the Christian gospel.

These schools seem to hold great promise for delivering children from the destructive competition so characteristic of state schools. Many of us assumed that Christian schools would veer away from those teaching techniques which have created negative self-images and feelings of personal failure for so many children. We thought that the Christian day school would allow children to be educated in a context that affirmed individual worth. We believed that children would not be pitted against each other in ways that created emotional alienation. We supposed the expectation that all children in a given age bracket should be able to accomplish the same things would be discarded. But for the most part, our hopes have not been realised.

In the best of Christian day schools, an attempt is made to integrate Christian teachings into the curriculum. Usually, biology is taught so that children see how God was involved in the development of life. Art and music teach the tremendous contributions of the people of God. History courses take into account the greatest event in the annals of recorded time—the life of Christ. In Christian schools the gospel story and the theology of the church are presented. But while the content of the educational process may be Christian, the way in which the children are taught is usually the same as in the state school system.

An ideal Christian school

What I long to see is the establishment of more Christian schools where the goals include not only communication of the message of Jesus, the accumulated knowledge of the society, and the development of the individual talents of the pupils, but also *an educational process that gives children feelings of deep personal worth, an awareness of their accomplishments, and feelings of success*. Such schools would shy away from standardised expectations for all children, recognising as Jesus does, that each child has unique gifts, traits, and abilities, and will develop at a rate different from his peers.

In such a school each child would be evaluated in terms of how well he was realising his own potential, rather than how he compared to others at the same age level. Success would no longer be dependent upon competitive comparisons, but rather on the degree to which the child was discovering and developing the gifts that God had given him.

A kibbutz school

A close approximation of the system being advocated has been developed in the State of Israel. The Jewish people have created a model for education that is worthy of some consideration by those of us trying to implement Christian principles into the educational process. I am, of course, referring to the Israeli kibbutz (a communal farm). As this system is analysed, I must enter a disclaimer: I am not advocating this system, only asking that we study some of its educational principles.

In one kibbutz I studied, the whole emphasis was to build a high level of solidarity among members and to work for the emotional adjustment of each child. The medium of education was designed to reach these goals. In the morning when the children arrived at school, they were expected to put on uniforms. The interesting thing about these uniforms was that the buttons were arranged in the back of the clothes, leaving the children in the strange predicament of not being able to fasten them by themselves. Each child had to depend on another pupil to help him dress and prepare for the experiences of the day. This was just one subtle means whereby children were taught to depend upon each other in a co-operative and helpful manner, rather than to view one another as competitors.

Another way that this kibbutz encouraged mutuality and interdependence was through play. All children enjoy building things with wooden blocks. However, in this kibbutz, the blocks were so heavy that a single child could not lift any of them. For the child to build anything, he would have to co-operate with one or two other children. By working together they could achieve what no one of them could alone.

Of particular interest to me was the educational process in the upper classes. There the pupils progressed only as fast as the slowest child could learn. When a test was given and one of the children failed, the class would then go back over the material until that child could successfully complete the examination. It was interesting to see how the other children in the class helped the slow one along in his studies. They had a vested interest in the slow child's accomplishments. They could not learn additional material until the material already taught was mastered by their slower friend. So they encouraged him and cheered his every accomplishment, and when he finally did comprehend the material, they made him feel that he had done something wonderful for all of them—and indeed he had.

This concern for the slower pupil is quite a contrast to the contempt that fast learners often show within our highly competitive learning system. If, as a slow student in spelling, I had been surrounded by encouragement and support from my peers instead of the put-down that I experienced from Mary and the others while playing spelling baseball, my whole self-concept might be different today.

This is not to suggest that the style of education in a kibbutz is problem-free. Bruno Bettelheim, one of America's leading psychologists, made careful studies of life in the kibbutz. He found that while it did much to diminish neurotic drives towards achievement and to help children gain a better acceptance of themselves as persons, the system left much to be desired. For instance, Bettlelheim pointed out that young people in the kibbutz often lacked the capability to make individualistic decisions; they lacked autonomy and often did not know how to function when each member was left on his own. Furthermore, Bettelheim discovered that the children of the kibbutz lacked long-range goals in life. They were so devoid of a drive for achievement that they seldom saw success as a goal for which present sacrifices should be made.

Competition is part of the real world in which children must eventually function. Long-range goals are necessary.

Undoubtedly, the kibbutz would not adequately prepare people to function in modern Britain. Nevertheless, efforts must be made to deliver children from the kind of destructive competition that is dehumanising.

If God has given us children to raise in the nurture and admonition of the Lord, we should be committed to developing all of the gifts within each child. Children need to see that in the competitive struggles which are part of school and play, the most important goal should be to surpass one's own previous achievements rather than to prove superiority over peers. We can help children love themselves because they sense their infinite worth and not because they do better than other children. Only those who love themselves properly can truly love Christ and other people. Developing this capacity in children is essential for the future of the nation and of the world.

5
Coming of Age

As a child moves into the teenage years, he feels an increasing need to be popular. In fact, there is a great likelihood popularity will become his ultimate goal.

To achieve this, the teenager in our modern culture develops what sociologist David Reisman calls an *other-directed personality*. He develops a sixth sense which enables him to pick up from any group what they expect from him. Once he has a reading on the group, he is able to conform to what he believes will gain him group approval.

It is fascinating to watch a teenager come into a new group. At first he simply observes, attempting not to reveal any of his own thoughts or feelings. He 'plays it cool', trying to communicate an air of detachment. Because he is careful not to respond with either enthusiasm or contempt to what the other members of the group are doing, his face may appear almost emotionless. He is 'playing it cool' to allow himself time to figure out what the members of the group expect him to be. Once he has 'the feel' of the group, he will gradually begin to behave in ways which he believes will earn him approval and acceptance.

It takes a long time to develop this sixth sense. Some young people never do and consequently, may be labelled as *weird* and *nerd*. There seems to be no end to the labels young people dream up for those individuals who miscalculate what the group expects of them, and do and say the wrong things with the wrong people. When a particular young person is guilty of this 'unforgivable sin', his peers usually say that he has 'blown it'. The horrible thing is that once the individual has blown it, there is not much he can do to set things right. Teenagers are very unforgiving; once they have defined an individual as a loser, he might as well give up, or try to achieve success with another group somewhere else.

Other-directed teens

Adult advisers who work with church youth groups need to remember that the behaviour of teenagers tends to be *other-directed*. When a young person comes to the meeting and sits there seemingly detached, emotionless, and even sullen, the youth leader may ask himself, 'Why does he come if he's not going to get anything out of it?' He comes because he wants to be accepted by the members of the group and to gain popularity in their eyes. He sits there looking detached and uninvolved because he hasn't yet figured out what will earn him that treasured approval.

At one time when I was the leader of a church youth group, I became very frustrated because my group wouldn't sing choruses that had always been such an enjoyment to me when I was their age. I was further perplexed because when I would take them to a youth rally where there were hundreds of other young people, they would then sing their lungs out. I'd ask myself, 'Why can't I get them to sing like that?'

The answer is that they sang with enthusiasm at the youth rally because they sensed that it was expected of them; they failed to sing at the small youth gathering because they were afraid they would look ridiculous in the eyes of their peers.

Group acceptance

Adults too easily forget how disastrous it is when a young person blows his chances for group acceptance. Should it take place in a church gathering, there is a strong probability that the young person will never come back to the church again. When this happens at secondary school, the pupil may not only withdraw from school activities, but may also long to move to a new town where he can start over again and have another chance at gaining acceptance by the 'in' crowd.

On occasion, I have seen rejection by the 'in' group at school result in tremendous dedication to the church. A young person who fails to 'make it' with the gang at school may become intensely committed to the church youth group if he finds a community of acceptance there that makes him feel worthwhile. Many a young person has come to Christ for that reason alone.

I do not want to question commitments to the church that are made on such grounds, but I would offer a reminder that involvement in the church youth group does not necessarily mean that the individual is committed to Christ. The two sometimes go together, but not always.

The church has always attracted society's losers because they can feel like winners within its fellowship. The early church grew because many people who were rejects in society found acceptance and affirmation within the community of believers.

But Christianity must go deeper than group affirmation if it is to be genuine. It must involve a person's relationship with the resurrected Christ. Because such a relationship is often communicated through a loving group, it is possible for an individual to love the church fellowship without loving Jesus.

The chameleon

It is easy for the other-directed personality to be superficial. His behaviour is not so much determined by inner conviction as it is by what other people expect. In each group he gets a reading of what is expected of him and accordingly conforms. These groups may have values and expectations that are vastly different from each other, but the completely other-directed person will be able to succeed in all of them. He simply alters his personality as he moves from group to group, so that with one set of associates he is one kind of person, while with another group he becomes entirely different.

For several years I was a faculty proctor, living in the men's hall of residence of a small Christian liberal arts college in the USA, where I got to know my students very well. One particular young man seemed to lack any semblance of Christian commitment. He had no time for the church or for the Bible study groups on campus, and he ridiculed those who took such things seriously. He often went drinking with friends at the local bar, and was sexually promiscuous.

One evening after I had spoken at a church, a middle-aged woman came to me and asked if I knew her son who was a student at my college. I knew him all right—he was the very boy I have described. The woman then went on to say, 'Isn't he a lovely boy? He is such a deeply committed Christian. When he's at home during the summer, he is a leader of the youth here at church. He conducts the Bible study at the midweek service when the pastor is away on holiday. Everyone at the church looks up to him and thinks I'm so lucky to have such a wonderful son.'

I immediately began to wonder if her boy and the young man I knew at college were one and the same person. The answer was Yes. He was other-directed. When he was at home with the church people, his behaviour was 'churchy', and when he was away at college, he sought the approval of a group with different values.

The German existentialist writer, Martin Heidegger, would have called him *inauthentic*. Jean-Paul Sartre would have said he was *guilty of non-being*.

We will simply call him an expression of David Reisman's other-directed personality. He was a young man who lacked any personal identity. By the end of each day, he had played so many different roles for so many different groups that he could legitimately look in the mirror and ask himself, 'Will the real me please step forward?'

When I returned to college, I met this young man in the entrance-hall of the main building, and said, 'Guess where I was last night? I was at the Lakeview Baptist Church.'

He said, 'That's my church!' I replied, 'I know, and Charlie, we both know what a phony you are. You're a completely different person at home with those church people, aren't you?' His head dropped, and shame seemed to overwhelm him.

The following term Charlie came straight to my office and said, 'Dr Campolo, remember that talk we had last year? Well, you were right; I was being phony. But it's different now. I want you to know that this summer I never attended church once.'

That wasn't exactly what I had in mind, but I would have to say that the young man was then closer to the kingdom of God than ever before. At least he knew that Christianity is not a style of behaviour one assumes when one is with Christian people, that it is more than saying the right words and doing the right things in the right setting. He had come to grips with what Christianity is not, and this might set him up for a confrontation with what Christianity is—a personal surrender to Jesus who guides from within, no matter where you are.

I am happy to report that I was able to lead this young man to a knowledge of Jesus Christ as Lord and Saviour, and that he is now living what I believe to be a consistent life for Christ. Many times I have thanked God for the opportunity to confront him with the incongruities of his life.

Need for individuality

Young people are aware of their tendencies to conform to the expectations of others. Many of them, deep down inside, condemn such conformity and crave to be individuals with the integrity to stand up to any group and to affirm their identity, regardless of what others might think. But they don't know how to be individualistic. Even in their attempts at nonconformity, they seem to be imitating others. The members of the rebellious youth culture often look alike, dress alike, and talk alike. Even in their rebellion, they are conforming to what they think will gain them acceptance with their counter-culture friends.

Young people need to see that social nonconformity has its most positive expression in becoming a Christian and being guided from within by the Holy Spirit. The apostle Paul wrote:

> I urge you therefore, brethren, by the mercies of God, to present your bodies a living and holy sacrifice, acceptable to God, which is your spiritual service of worship. And do not be conformed to this world, but be transformed by the renewing of your mind, that you may prove what the will of God is, that which is good and acceptable and perfect (Rom 12:1–2).

Or, as J.B. Phillips translates these verses:

> With eyes wide open to the mercies of God, I beg you, my brothers, as an act of intelligent worship, to give him your bodies, as a living sacrifice, consecrated to him and acceptable by him. Don't let the world around you squeeze you into its own mould, but let God re-mould your minds from within, so that you may prove in practice that the plan of God for you is good, meets all his demands and moves towards the goal of true maturity.

Young people need to understand that if they invite Jesus into their lives, the influence he will exert on their behaviour from within will be greater than that exerted on them by the expectations of others. In Christ is the source of true individuality.

6

Teenage Success with the Opposite Sex

Success for young people is tied to gaining the approval of their peers. And of all the members of their peer groups, those of the opposite sex loom as the most significant. Most boys want to be approved by girls, and girls want to gain recognition from the boys.

Popularity with the opposite sex can make young people feel that they have achieved what is most important in life. Also, they are seen as successful in the eyes of their peers. This means that the boy who is successful with girls will be admired by his male companions, and the girl who is successful with the boys will gain admiration from her female friends.

The boy who can date the most sought-after girls has achieved the ultimate status symbol in the youth subculture. The girl who has so many boys chasing her that she has to beat them off is the envy of most other girls. She finds that even her parents take pride in her popularity with boys. The importance of dating in the teenage culture cannot be exaggerated. The dating game is played for stakes that are too high for most of us older folks to remember very well.

The teenage boy

There are several marks of success—as seen by a teenage boy.

1. Humour. The adolescent male is convinced that to be successful with girls he must have a good personality. In the teenage subculture that means 'being funny'. He will try hard to be funny and to entertain everyone with his jokes. Unfortunately, it takes years to become witty and to develop sophisticated humour. This means that the average teenager often ends up making a fool of himself. Sometimes he tells bad jokes which inflict pain on others. Being funny is so important that he might even try to get a cheap laugh by ridiculing someone who seems to be a bit weird to his crowd. If all else fails, an off-colour joke can be used to get the gang laughing. He knows that most of his friends are afraid not to laugh at dirty jokes for fear that they will be considered immature. And what could be worse for a teenager than to have his friends consider him immature?

I am not trying to excuse any of this behaviour. Rather, I want you to understand it and have some pity for the boy who is trying too hard to be funny. Youth leaders need to be prepared for the struggling teenager who continuously disrupts the meetings with inane remarks.

When I was in my teens, being funny was so important that I seldom gave consideration to how my 'humour' affected others. One of the 'funny' things my friends and I did was associated with driving our buddy Billy Turner home after a basketball game. It would be about midnight when we drove up to his terraced house. As he got out of the car, we would honk the horn and scream at the top of our lungs. 'Hey, Mrs Turner, here comes your drunken son'. The driver would then step on the gas, spin his wheels, and with the screech of spinning rubber we would zoom away. By this time Billy Turner's neighbours would be awake and his parents angry. We all thought this was very funny.

The practical joker who gets a laugh at another person's expense is omnipresent in the teenage world. He may pull out the chair behind you as you sit down, or loosen the tops on the salt pots in the cafeteria; he has an endless array of such tricks. Being funny is his way to popularity.

2. *Possessions*. Another route taken by teenage boys seeking status—and girls too—is purchasing the right consumer goods. Jules Henry, the famous anthropologist, has pointed out that we live in a consumer society where one gains status by possessing the right things. A boy thinks if he wears the right clothes, drives the right car, listens to the right kind of records, and plays them on the right kind of stereo, people will think he's 'really with it'.

Possessing the right things *does* gain some status in the youth subculture, and young people know it. Parents find themselves constantly being nagged by their children, who seem to have an unending list of things that cost too much money. Although parents get exasperated over these materialistic demands, they should understand that their children want these things in order to gain the acceptance that possessing them may bring.

3. *Sports*. Another way for males to achieve popularity in the youth culture is through sports. I remember being willing to do almost anything in my teenage years to make the school basketball team. I knew that being on the team would gain me instant status with males and females alike. For endless hours I practised my jump shot, constantly fantasising about scoring the winning basket for my school against its arch rival. The scene was always the same: I saw myself stealing the ball and shooting a jump shot from at least twenty feet out, while the crowd roared in excitement and the final gun went off, just as the ball swished through the net. I imagined a voice broadcasting in the background, 'Campolo steals the ball, dribbles to the top of the key—leaps into the air—he lets go of the jump shot—IT'S GOOD!'

In my fantasy this was always followed by the roar of the crowd. But most important of all was that the girls, including that special girl, were impressed.

Sports can be valuable, but not when they become the primary means in a struggle for popularity. We kid ourselves into thinking that it is good clean body-building and sports-manship that are being developed in school athletics. A great deal of what goes on in the name of sports is an attempt for males to gain recognition, particularly from females. There is nothing wrong with popularity, but there is something wrong when all of a youth's activities are aimed at achieving that one goal.

4. *Talking big*. Having the right things, making the team, pulling off the right stunts mean very little unless the 'right' people know about them. Consequently, every boy must master the technique of letting other people know about him without seeming like a braggart. As a young person, I partic-ularly liked those occasions when I was away from home for the summer holidays. If I was at a camp 100 miles from home, I felt that I had an opportunity to gain status simply by 'talk-ing big'. I exaggerated my limited athletic accomplishments until I was a superstar. I would talk of what I owned, places I had been, and things I had done. And I did so with a style that I believed would convince them I was incredibly won-derful. I remember being afraid that someone might learn the truth about me. I never wanted any of them to visit me when camp was over lest they learn the reality that I was just an ordinary kid. Sometimes I shuddered at the thought of being found out.

The tendency to exaggerate exploits in order to build an image bigger than life is characteristic of most boys, but it is never more evident than in those crucial teenage years when gaining popularity with one's peers—and particularly the girls—is of ultimate importance. Young people often feel guilty over these deceptions and are afraid that they will be found out. By exaggerating, the young person is really sug-gesting that he is not worthy to be liked as he is and must appear to be something different in order to be popular. This behaviour is evidence of self-rejection. If only he could be more than he is!

The teenage girl

The need to be successful at dating is even more urgent for girls than for boys. Many girls feel as if they are nothing if they fail to attract the kind of dates they desperately want. However, a girl faces special problems because of society's demands.

1. *Good looks for self-esteem.* For the female trying to succeed at the dating game, the most important attribute is 'good looks'. It won't do to tell the teenage girl that 'looks aren't everything'. She knows better. She realises that boys don't pay much attention to those who are physically unattractive. She knows that girls who are unattractive are referred to as 'plain Jane' by the boys. One consequence of living in a sexist society is that a female may have personality, depth of character, wit, intelligence and untold positive traits. But she doesn't stand much of a chance without an attractive face and a well-shaped body.

The female who fails to measure up to the appearance prescribed by society often finds that not even her family will provide her with a positive self-image. Parents tend to view their children as they think other teenagers see them. I have seen mothers brag about their daughters by pointing out the fact that their daughters have more dates than they can handle. Some mothers believe that their daughters are beautiful if they get a lot of dates, and I have known mothers who define their daughters as unattractive because those girls are ignored by boys.

One summer when I was lecturing at the University of Pennsylvania, a very attractive woman came into the lecture and took her place in the front row. By any definition she would have to be described as stunning. In fact, she was so attractive that her very presence became a distraction in my small group. The students and I usually had lunch together, and we got to know each other quite well. In the course of our many discussions, it became obvious that this young woman had a very low self-concept. She didn't believe herself to be worth anything and seemed to have no idea how beautiful she was.

We couldn't understand the source of her low self-esteem until one day she passed around some high school photographs. Suddenly we understood. In high school she had been plump, her dress and her hairstyle had been out of fashion and she had looked very plain. She had probably been dateless and had developed a very negative self-image. In her early twenties her body had shaped into what this culture calls attractive. She had learned how to dress fashionably, and her face had matured into beauty; but it was too late. She was stuck with an earlier self-image but would not change, in spite of what she had become.

A few years later, while in Manhatten, I stepped into a bar just off Times Square looking for a telephone. There, sitting on a bar stool looking for a pick-up, was my former student. My heart sank and I turned away so as not to embarrass her by my recognition. She is just one example of what can happen to those girls who lose out with the boys in their teenage years. The system made my student feel worthless, and she behaved in ways that reflected a poor self-image.

2. *The trauma of school dances.* The emotional brutality that females must endure in the dating game became clear to me when I was still in high school. During my last year I was elected president of the student council. That was a real ego trip and everyone was happy for me. The pastor of my church patted me on the back and told me that this was an opportunity to be 'a real testimony for Jesus'. (I have never understood why the church thinks that those who are socially successful have the testimonies most worth hearing. The Lord does equally exciting work among those whom the world rejects.)

To my surprise, I discovered that one of my responsibilities as student council president was to set up a dance for the student body each month. My problem was that I belonged to one of those churches which taught that dancing was wrong.

My pastor said, 'It stimulates the lust of the flesh.' There is undoubtedly truth to what he said, as any observation of a dance will support, but I doubt that what goes on at most school dances is any worse than what goes on at most church parties.

In any event, I resolved the dilemma of fulfilling my responsibilities as student council president, while remaining faithful to the expectations of my church, by setting up the dance, being present when it took place, but *not* dancing. This afforded me a detachment from the dance that allowed me to observe what was going on.

The decorating committee and I got to the school gym about 6:30 in the evening. We opened the windows to air the place because the basketball team had just finished practising. Next we got out the crepe paper, which was always used to decorate for such occasions, and strung it across the room. At 7 pm Roger showed up. I was surprised to see him because he wasn't the kind of boy I thought would have much success with the girls in such a setting. He was a bit strange and had not developed those other-directed traits that would have enabled him to fit in with his peers. He was awkward and lanky. Under Roger's right arm were records, and I immediately knew what he was going to do. All evening he would be the one who would sit up on the stage changing records and keeping the music going so others could dance.

Playing the records was Roger's way of participating in the dance without getting hurt, and yet he was hurting. I knew he was hurting. When the teacher who was serving as a chaperone told me that she thought everyone was having a good time, I was positive that she had not given proper consideration to poor Roger.

Around the four walls of the gym, we arranged folding chairs. That evening about fifty girls were sitting on them with bored looks of indifference. I watched them as they put on an air of sophistication and pretended that they were really above what was happening on the dance floor. But their facade of nonchalance was only an attempt to cover up the anxieties and fears they had, as they sat there wondering whether or not they would be asked to dance. They were hoping with all their might that they would not end up as total rejects. They suffered in quiet desperation but knew that they dared not show it.

After the dance was over, I was standing out on 48th Street in front of West Philadelphia High, when my lab partner, came running out of the school. She was a special girl, undoubtedly the wittiest person I knew. Besides that, she had a kindness and sweetness about her that made her a joy to all who knew her. As she ran past me I yelled in my friendliest manner 'Hi!'

She didn't answer and that was so unlike her. She jumped into a waiting car and before her father could drive her away from the kerb, I watched my friend Mary break down and cry. I felt angry with the whole scene and decided then and there that I would never take part in another school dance.

My opposition to dances did not stem from the belief that relates to the lust of the flesh. Instead, it stemmed from the hurt that I saw so many endure.

3. *Perennial rejects.* I have only been describing the hurt experienced by those who came to the dance. I cannot imagine what it was like for the greater proportion of the student body who stayed at home that evening because they knew what would happen if they came. They did not want to subject themselves to that kind of possible rejection. How hard it must have been for them when their mothers asked, 'Why don't you go to the dance tonight and have a good time?'

What does one answer? 'I'm a reject'? 'I'm a loser?' 'I'm a nothing'?

Perhaps a well-meaning father will 'drive the final nails into the coffin' as he says in love, 'I know—let's all go out together this evening.'

It is no wonder that the teenager often answers angrily, 'Why don't you leave me alone?'

Of course, dating is not destructive for everyone. There are many young people who go out and have good times. However, parents should warn them that the dating game as a whole, and the dance in particular, are deceiving. The dating game leads people to think that the traits which make them successful in these activities are the ones that really matter in life. The truth is that these traits don't matter very much in the adult world.

Few things are as pathetic as watching a middle-aged woman trying to look and act like a teenager. As she senses that the traits that made her successful in those earlier days are slipping away, she tries desperately to hold onto them. She doesn't dress or act her age because she feels so threatened by having lost those attributes which made her the queen of the local carnival. Most of the traits which make for success in attracting attention and dating will not help much in real life.

A university student, after hearing one of my lectures condemning the dating game, gave me this poem.

Ode to a Pretty Girl
Pretty girl
when you walk by
our eyes measure your breasts
and if you show us skin
our mouths will salivate
while our minds hallucinate
about you.

You are the girl of our dreams
but you are a nightmare
to yourself.
For how will you ever be sure
Why he whispers in your ear, 'I love you'?

Don't be angry at us.
He—we—cannot help
ourselves.

This lust for you
comes from within—
a seed planted by our
parents and their friends and enemies
who all got together
in harmony
to do this evil thing.

It is a reflex.
We do not deliberate
when we envision you
in our arms.
It is there (Now).

But you will enjoy your curse
for you will never be bored
you never will be alone
but Always, Always
you shall be lonely.
You can fool yourself sometimes,
and he can fool you too
because he is trained to do that
and you too are trained
and we are all trained
to fool each other
to fool ourselves
to live a lie.

And if anyone ever seeks the Truth
he will be mocked!
And if anyone ever finds the Truth
he will be isolated!
And if anyone ever tells the Truth
he will be killed!

so that everyone else can live a lie
in Peace.

Remember, pretty girl,
a sad search for Truth is better than
contentment with what is false.
There's no such thing as
Love without Truth
and, perhaps, if you seek Truth
you will find Love.

Particular temptations for a Christian girl

The Christian girl faces a host of temptations while playing the dating game. Indeed, the circumstances surrounding dating probably pose the greatest threat to the maintenance of her Christian commitment. I am not simply referring to the notion that some young people feel that they have to let down their sexual standards in order to gain popularity with the opposite sex. This may not be as true as a lot of people think it is.

1. *Dates with non-Christians.* Most likely the greatest temptation will be to date those who aren't Christians and to develop deep relationships with them. Young people sometimes feel they are not worth much of anything unless they date. This kind of thinking leads to a willingness to settle for less than they should in areas of lasting importance. I know that it may seem narrow-minded to suggest that Christians should only date Christians. But nothing has greater potential for destroying a young girl's Christian commitment than a dating relationship with someone who doesn't share her faith.

The apostle Paul says, 'Do not be bound together with unbelievers' (2 Cor 6:14). While the young girl may argue that she doesn't intend to marry the guy she's dating, her claim of 'not being serious' is a bit naive. Dating is much more serious than most people think. The emotions during the dating period are intense, and dating arrangements often do lead to marriage. Many women have told me that they dated their husbands 'just for fun', never intending to marry them because they weren't Christians. But they did end up together and the marriages have been less than completely happy.

2. *Playing dumb.* There is still another reason why dating tends to threaten the female's Christianity. In order to be good date bait, a female often has to pretend that she is less intelligent than she really is. Our world is filled with male chauvinists. Insecure males feel threatened by women who are very bright. Consequently, females often tend to play down their intelligence in order to entice males to like them. Few things upset me more than watching an intelligent woman conceal her brains for fear of losing out in the competition for dates.

At college, I find that females tend to do better in written tests and examinations than males. Yet, in spite of their obvious grasp of the material, these women very seldom participate in student discussions. They will sit there demurely, while males with half their knowledge take over the debate. It bothers me to have to listen to asinine statements from some of my male students when I know that females who have much more to contribute will not speak out.

Traditionally, teenage females have refused to pursue the most prestigious professions for fear that their accomplishments might make them losers in the quest for marriage partners. Some choose to be nurses when they should be doctors. Others aim to be secretaries when they should be executives.

When females become less than they can be, they are failing the Lord. When God created us, he gave us definite potentialities. If we fail to become all that he created us to be, we are guilty of sin. It is interesting to note that in the Greek New Testament the word for sin is *hamartia*, which means, 'to miss the mark'. The New Testament suggests that *sin* is failing to become all that you can be. This means that when a female fails to realise her highest potential because she is afraid to threaten the weak ego of an insecure male, she has compromised her faith.

Some will argue that I am overstating the case: they will contend that the dating game does not inflict anywhere near the amount of pain that I suggest. If you are among those who are sceptical about my assertions, let me remind you that just a couple of years ago a leading song on the hit parade in both Britain and the USA was about the agonies of a dateless teenage girl. The lyrics of 'At Seventeen' describe that suffering eloquently. A few phrases from the song express the pain of the girl who waits for what never comes to her: 'ravaged faces', 'inventing lovers', 'dubious integrity', 'ugly duckling girls', 'cheat ourselves,' and 'ugly girls like me'.

The song became popular because countless teenage girls on both sides of the Atlantic identified with its message. It became such a massive hit because it articulated miseries that were too deep for them to express.

The church and dating

The church has failed to understand the desperate needs of young people who are buying into the success goals of society. Also, the church has paid very little attention to what is at stake in the dating game. Christians have felt content if they could keep the youth of the church sexually 'pure' during the crucial teenage years. Young people have heard sermons and fireside chats on the necessity for sexual purity, but they seldom hear anything to help them work through the more complex problems related to dating. There is much that the church might do to help teenagers in these matters, and I would like to make a few suggestions.

The church should sponsor no activity that requires a partner of the opposite sex in order to participate. The world functions in a way that often excludes certain people and makes them feel like rejects, but the church should never do this.

I have always liked sponsored walks where young people

look for sponsors to pay them a certain amount of money for each mile they walk for a worthy cause. The thing I like best about such group walks is that the basis for participation is not sexual attractiveness, but rather an altruistic concern for other people.

During sponsored walks, young people often enjoy long talks with one another. Many times those who don't appear very special at the start become more attractive during the conversation and walk. Isn't it fascinating how the ways that people appear to us are altered as we get to know them in depth? Some friends that I now think are the most beautiful seemed plain to me when I first met them. And some whom I thought to be stunning on first appearance proved less than attractive after a lengthy encounter.

Bike hikes, progressive suppers, tenpin bowling, and many other activities can be all-inclusive. If you feel you are rather lacking in bright ideas, don't worry. Plenty of books have been written to help you and should be available from your local Christian bookshop. Among them are *The Christian Youth Manual* by Steve Chalke (Kingsway, 1987/1992), *Youth Work Ideas!* by John Buckeridge (Kingsway, 1993), and *Big Ideas for Small Youth Groups* by Patrick Angier and Nick Aiken (Marshall Pickering, 1992).

Above all else, it is necessary for Christians to communicate to young people the good news about Jesus. They must come to see that Jesus accepts them just as they are. They don't have to make any team or do some great deed or be beautiful. They are loved infinitely and appreciated intensely for what they are. Young people desperately need the message that acceptance by Jesus is not something which needs to be earned.

7
Symptoms of Midlife Males

The average male wins success primarily through his vocation. His status, income, and ability to exercise power over others are all wrapped up with his occupation. It is even safe to say that vocation is usually the means whereby male identity is achieved.

When a man meets a stranger, usually the first question asked of him is, 'What do you do for a living?' People evaluate him and define his social significance when they learn his vocation. Since an individual's self-concept is largely based on what he feels significant others think of them, such a definition of social significance has great importance.

Because the male's social identify is so tied to his vocation, it is important for us to be reminded that there can be a difference between what a person *is* and what he *does*. What a person *is* is usually so much deeper and more significant than what he *does* that knowing his vocation may give only a hint of his true identity.

Christians should know better than to evaluate the significance of a person totally in terms of his vocation. We are supposed to be people who do not live according to our sinful nature but according to the Spirit (Rom 8:4). This means that we do not use the same criteria as society does to evaluate individuals. Unfortunately, Christians do not always live in accord with the Scripture's admonition. In an overwhelming number of churches, the tendency is to evaluate people in much the same way as the secular world evaluates them.

Imagine a Sunday morning at at typical church. A new couple comes in and finds a place to sit in one of the pews. In a small church, most of the congregation will wonder who they are, and the pastor will pay special attention to them as he sits with his posed reverence on the pulpit chair. As soon as the service is over, some church members will make sure that the new couple feels welcome. Some of the key members will immediately surround them and ask 'What's your name?' The second question, probably aimed at the man, will be 'What do you do?'

If he tells them that he is the newly appointed teacher at the local secondary school, you can imagine the response. Someone will wave over the Sunday school superintendent and whisper, 'He's the new teacher at Kingsbury School.' The superintendent is likely to shoot a quick prayer up to the Lord, 'Thank thee, Jesus. That class of thirteen-year-olds hast wiped out four teachers in a row and lo, thou has provided still another.' The elated conversation will probably end with someone saying, 'If you haven't found a church home, we certainly hope that you make this your church. We could really *use* you.'

The man's vocation has been the basis for evaluation, and he has been approved because he can be *used* in the work of the church. No one knows if he loves Christ or is committed to Christian service or if he has a grasp of the Scriptures.

Erich Fromm once said that the problem with our age is that we love things and use people instead of using things and loving people. Maybe the church could take a page from the writings of this great humanist. We should be considering people in terms of how we can love them, not in terms of how we might use them.

Prestige versus person

It is interesting to note that Jesus did not choose his disciples from among those who held prestigious positions in society. Instead, he chose a couple of fishermen, a tax collector (they were bad people in those days), and two troublemakers who were called the 'Sons of Thunder'. Some of the women who followed Jesus were unimpressive, and one had a reputation so low that people murmured against the Lord for associating with her.

Christ looked within people and tried to discern their hungers, dreams, and values, and ultimately, their faith. In our hurried age, we haven't the time to gain an in-depth analysis of persons. We meet people casually and want some quick and simple way to judge them. And too often we evaluate them according to vocation.

Sociologists have studied our system of stratifying people and have compiled a list of vocations in accord with the prestige that we assign to them. Starting from the top, we give priority to occupations in the following order: professional and technical workers; farmers and farm managers; managers and administrators, except farm; clerical workers; sales workers; craftsmen, foremen; operatives; private household workers; service workers, except private household; farm labourers, nonfarm labourers

Those who have vocations near the top of this list are often very impressed with their own success and desire to impress others with their roles in society. To make sure that strangers quickly find out what they do, some people in these professions try to manipulate conversations so that they can talk about their prominence.

Once I was at a party with a friend who is a medical doctor. Since I was the only one he knew at the gathering, he stayed close to me. It was interesting to watch and listen as he entered into conversations with various people throughout the evening. For some reason they were failing to ask him what he did for a living and that upset him. I watched him become increasingly anxious as he tried to work into the conversations hints about his profession, hoping that when people realised he was a doctor they would respect him. He became so deliberate that by the end of the evening I felt that he was about to stand on a chair and yell, 'Look at me! I'm a doctor! Why aren't you impressed?'

While no one is denying the importance of vocation, as Christians we know that many people who have prestigious vocations are hollow and superficial. On the other hand, many individuals whose vocational status is not highly ranked by society prove to possess spiritual qualities which make them great people to know.

When my boy was eight, he came home and explained that his homework that day was to prepare a talk on the topic, 'What I want to be when I grow up.'

I told him, 'Tell your teacher that when you grow up you want to be a fully realised human being like Jesus. Tell her that what she meant to ask was what you want to *do* to earn money.' He told her, and it didn't go down well at all.

It is important to impress on children that in the Christian value system, being a successful person is far more important than having a prestigious vocation. Christians should realise that it is possible for people to have a deep sense of success, even when the world is unimpressed by them. And vice versa, it is possible for people to awe society with their accomplishments but inwardly to feel like failures.

Prestige for the family

Married men know that their vocations determine not only their own positions in society, but also provide status for their wives and children. They know that their children will gain prestige among their friends if they can brag about what their fathers do. So much is the social standing of children connected with the successes of their fathers that children will often argue among themselves as to whose father has the most important job.

Women are also conscious of the fact that their status is tied to their husbands' vocations. When they marry, many women give careful consideration to the vocation of potential partners, for they know that their places in society will be determined by the social positions of their husbands.

We all know women who have driven their husbands to become successful because that success would reflect on them. Shakespeare's Lady Macbeth was not the only woman in history guilty of self-interest as she expressed ambition for her husband.

One of the cries of modern feminists is that women should be free to determine their places in society through their own achievements. If the feminists succeed, some men might experience welcome relief from the pressures of wives ambitious for vicarious success.

Midlife crisis

A society in which vocational achievement is the most important indicator of success is an ideal environment for a condition known as the 'midlife crisis'. This usually hits a man sometime after he passes the age of forty. The rapid succession of promotions of earlier years has slowed down, and he feels that he is not going anywhere. As he watches the younger people in his profession who seem to be moving ahead of him, he knows that he is no longer viewed as the promising executive. Rather, he has become an established bureaucrat, nervously protecting his job against the assaults of the 'young Turks'. In these middle years, the self-confidence that formerly verged on arrogance is dramatically shaken.

Middle-aged men who feel that they are not sufficiently appreciated by their companies often develop resentments towards people who gain the positions that they themselves desired. Feeling threatened and hurt, they often react with pettiness, attaching great importance to every symbol of prestige. The size of another man's desk, the kind of office equipment, the location of the office, the amount of secretarial help—all can take on exaggerated importance. It is not so much a need for these things as that these symbols provide desperately needed assurances of personal importance. It is pathetic to see a once proud man bickering over such trifles.

Sometimes these threatened males have their greatest fears realised, as jobs are phased out. When men in the middle years suddenly find that their services are no longer required, their egos are shattered and their self-confidence is gone. Often their personal wealth is diminished and like Willie Loman in Arthur Miller's play, *Death of a Salesman*, they see little left to live for.

It is hard for a throwaway executive or unemployed factory worker not to feel contempt for himself. He sold himself to the demands of the job, tailoring his personality to the expectations of his role. He compromised his personal integrity in order to fit the expectations of 'the organisation man'. He said the right things, held the proper political views, attended the right church, and joined the right golf club in his effort to establish the proper image. Having become what he thought his company wanted, he now feels betrayed.

Sören Kierkegaard once said, 'When a man aspires to be a Caesar and fails to become a Caesar, he will hate what he is because he is not a Caesar.' He meant that the man who fails to achieve what he set out to achieve will end up hating himself.

Fortunately, most men do not lose their jobs during the midlife crisis. But even those who remain employed often find their jobs increasingly meaningless and come home emotionally dissipated at the end of the day. Paul Goodman, a prominent social critic of the 1960s, pointed out that there has never been a time in world history when men have worked less hard and come home more tired. That tiredness is not from physical exertion but from the emotional emptiness of not doing anything that seems worthwhile.

Escape routes at midlife

Men choose from a variety of escape routes, trying to bypass the depressions of midlife.

1. *Sports*. It is frightening to see a middle-aged man devoting large segments of his life to vicariously experiencing the thrill of stardom with his favourite sports personalities. He has little time for conversation, in-depth relationships, or the simple joys of family life because his life is consumed with being a television spectator. 'The thrill of victory and the agony of defeat' are larger in his consciousness than the thrills and agonies of his own experience or that of his family. His own existence becomes less real to him than that of his favourite sportsmen. He knows more about the personal lives of athletes than he does about what is going on in the lives of his own children. His emotional state is often determined by whether his favourite teams win or lose. Sometimes such a man will become so depressed when his favourite team loses that he commits suicide.

Evangelical Christians who frown on 'the pleasures of the world' often fail to see the destructive potential in the preoccupation with sports. While sports may provide wholesome fun for Christians, in more situations than we would like to admit, sports can also eat up precious time leaving people with little room in their lives for personal relationships or Christian service.

We must recognise that intense devotion to sports can become idolatrous, taking the place of God. This is certainly the case for the man who finds sports to be an escape from the meaninglessness of his everyday existence.

2. *Consumerism*. Another false escape route from the midlife crisis is found in buying things. We live in a consumer-orientated society. The ads on television attempt to convince us that we can gain a sense of meaning and fulfilment by purchasing the right things. There used to be a beer ad in America that played on our awareness of life slipping away: 'You

only go through life once, so why not reach for the gusto?' Of course, the ad promised that gusto could be gained by purchasing a six-pack of beer. Reflecting personal insecurities, another beer ad tells us, 'You tell the world you know what you're doing…'

Soft drinks are sold on the basis that they will make us young. The ads for men's clothing claim that success is tied to wearing the right styles and colours.

We do not need to look at *Top Gear* to be convinced that cars provide us with far more than a means of transport. They have become symbolic statements of who we are. An individual is saying something to the world when he drives a Mercedes Benz.

Within the context of such a consumer-oriented society, it is no surprise that many people meet the midlife crisis by buying more and more things. They hope to silence the gnawing awareness that they have failed to become what they hoped to be.

This escape route often has disastrous effects, as people extend their credit and mortgage their futures. Even Christians, who should know better, have bought piles of things that they really didn't need, in an attempt to drive out their feelings of emptiness and failure.

Society has facilitated this tendency to self-destruction by providing credit cards and easy loans to people whose buying habits have become a sickness. The church must prophetically declare that the media are wrong. In spite of what the ads declare, people cannot buy their way out of a sense of worthlessness. A great sadness comes when a person senses that failure in his vocation cannot be driven away by purchasing things. A voice still echoes down the corridors of time, saying 'Why do you spend…your wages for what does not satisfy?' (Isa 55:2).

3. *Work*. Some males deal with their midlife uncertainties by becoming workaholics. If they work twelve to eighteen hours a day, they never have to reflect upon their emotional

state. Blaise Pascal once said, 'All evil stems from this—that men do not know how to handle solitude.' What Pascal was trying to tell us is that in solitude, men are forced to reflect upon the meaning of their own lives. In solitude they are forced to come to grips with who they are and what they have become. Many men fill their lives with work so that they do not have to confront such solitude.

Most workaholics tend to make their jobs too important, attaching fantastic significance to every little thing they do. If their work is of great importance, then they must be important. They often become so bogged down in the imagined significance of trivia that their jobs become too much for them. For this reason, workaholism is usually self-defeating.

What the workaholic fears most is not death, but times of reflection in which he sees what he has become. Kierkegaard says we are like smooth pebbles thrown over the surface of a lake. We dance along the surface until we run out of momentum and then sink to a hundred thousand fathoms of nothingness. The workaholic knows that he cannot go on working for ever. Sooner or later, he must stop; work is only a temporary escape from nothingness.

4. *Children.* Many children find themselves pushed to achievement by fathers who try to live through the successes of their offspring, and so escape their own failures.

My boy is a member of his high school basketball team. The father of a player on his team came to every practice to watch his son go through the workouts and drills. The other boys became aware that his father was trying to live through his boy. My son joked about the man until one day he realised that the boy himself was painfully aware of what his father was doing.

5. *Affairs.* One of the most disastrous escape routes from the midlife crisis is the extramarital affair. Such an affair is particularly alluring if the partner is a younger woman, because the man is temporarily assured that he is not over the hill, but is still young enough to believe in his future. His own

wife knows him too well and urges him towards the reality of what he has become. Since the new younger woman doesn't know him well, she can help him play a game of make-believe. She serves a useful purpose as she becomes his significant other, reflecting to him an image of the mature power figure he always wanted to be. Even though she perpetrates a myth, he loves it.

It is important to note that it is the way she makes him *feel* that attracts him. He doesn't really love her—he is too empty to love anyone. When she no longer serves his purpose, he will drop her and look for somebody else to give him emotional support. Few are so vulnerable to extramarital affairs as men who are experiencing the midlife crisis. Even as far back as the Kinsey study, the evidence was clear that among middle-class men, the tendency towards extramarital affairs was most pronounced in their early forties.

Christian men often have sufficient grounding in the teachings of Scripture so as not to become sexually involved outside of marriage. However, many such men who would never 'touch' a woman can become emotionally involved with extramarital partners in ways that can prove to be dehumanising to their wives, and deceptive to themselves. Time and time again, I have counselled men who have not been sexually unfaithful, but who have allowed women other than their wives to become their significant others. This is a very common practice among clergymen, who often find in their congregations attractive younger women who are escaping from their own empty lives through romantic fantasies. Such arrangements are often clothed in phony nobility, as the partners blasphemously suggest that it is their loyalty to Christ that keeps them from going to bed together. In their pretence of Christlike behaviour, they massage each others' egos, at the expense of their respective spouses.

Once a woman sat crying in my office as she told me that her husband was having an affair. I asked her if she had any evidence of this—did she find a note, lipstick on the collar, or a motel slip? She quickly responded by saying 'Oh, I think I could survive the knowledge that my husband was keeping a whore on the side as long as I knew that I was his companion and partner; but it's the other way around. That other woman is his companion and partner and I am his whore!'

The husband in this story was a prominent Christian leader who had dehumanised his wife by making her into a sex partner, while denying her the intimacy of companionship and partnership in life. In a legalistic sense he had not committed adultery, but one wonders how many times while having sex with his wife, he had imagined himself with the other woman.

It is amazing how cruel Christians can be while pretending to uphold the letter of God's Law. No wonder Jesus pointed out that even if a man does not sleep with a woman, he still may be committing adultery with her in his fantasies.

This escape route leads nowhere. It is only a matter of time before the new arrangement loses its value as an escape from meaninglessness. Then the man will have to move on to another affair, as he seeks to buttress his faltering ego. Like Don Juan, he failed to see that the absence of lasting gratification is not in his sexual partner but in his own inadequacy.

8

Hope for the
Forty-three-Year-Old Man

The first step towards overcoming the midlife crisis is for a man to keep himself in good health, and well-rested. Middle-aged men need to realise that they can no longer physically exert themselves as they did when they were twenty-five years old, that they tire more quickly and need their rest. It is amazing how much more easily I can manage my life when I have eaten properly and had enough sleep. Men in their forties need holiday time to psychologically recuperate from the stress of their everyday lives. Unfortunately, not everyone can go to the French Riviera to get himself together again. But for those who can afford it, such a trip is worth the money, and could be less expensive than paying a psychiatrist. The mind and the body are intricately related and when the body is worn out, the mind is affected.

Chance of perspective

The midlife crisis should encourage a man to re-examine his life, to clarify his values, and to look at what he has achieved. It's a time to determine priorities and decide what should be of ultimate significance in life. Sometimes men find that when they consider what is *really* important and what is *relatively* important, they have nothing about which to be depressed and much for which to give thanks.

83

A sense of failure may result from a man's perspective on life. If he changes that perspective, he may feel like a different man. It is even possible for him to look at this job in a new way and to find real significance in his work.

Christopher Wren, the architect who designed so many of the great churches of London, told of walking through the building of St Paul's Cathedral, asking the various workers what they were doing. One explained that he was doing carpentry work, another that he was laying bricks, still another that he was putting stained-glass windows into place, and a fourth claimed to be carving stone. As he left the cathedral, Wren came upon a man mixing mortar and asked him what he was doing. The mason, not recognising the architect, proudly responded, 'Sir, I am building a great cathedral.'

However others might have described this man's work was of little consequence. By the grace of God, he was able to see his labour as a service to the Lord and to humanity. For him the mundane took on a sacred quality, giving his task new significance.

Change of occupation

Unfortunately, for most men this change of perspective doesn't help. In spite of efforts to find meaning, they come away from their labour with a sense of having wasted their lives. To such men, I can say, 'Why not consider a change?'

The middle years might prove to be a good time to change your job and go into something that offers a new challenge. I have seen men whose lives were routinised into boredom, who had lost their sense of aliveness, be emotionally reborn by changing jobs and doing something that they had always dreamed of doing.

I know some men in their early forties who have gone back to college in order to prepare for the ministry. I lecture part time at a Bible college and find that my best students are the middle-aged men who, during a midlife crisis, decided to become servants of the church. The dean of our college feels that these are the men who make the best pastors. They go into churches knowing the complexities that so many members of the congregation face, and which younger pastors cannot possibly comprehend.

A recent example of a radical midlife change is Chuck Colson. Many people refuse to accept what has happened to this Watergate conspirator. In his forties, crushed by his own mistakes, he discovered that he could find meaning in a life of Christian service. He has developed an organisation which provides special ministries to men and women who are in prison. Colson has created a life of significance out of personal disaster.

Albert Schweitzer at the age of forty had achieved fame as one of the great interpreters of Bach, had written a book that became a theological classic among students throughout the world, and was a wealthy man. Schweitzer was successful in the eyes of the world, but he did not feel fulfilled. At the age of forty he left it all for the interior of equatorial Africa to serve as a missionary. One doesn't have to agree with the theology of Albert Schweitzer to admire his commitment to service.

If you have approached your work in a Christlike spirit, endeavouring to find meaning in your labour, but are receiving no satisfaction from what you are doing, I would advise you to change jobs. I don't know where God wants you to be, but I know that God *does not* want you to be in a job that denies you fulfilment or diminishes your humanity. God created you in his image and, like your Lord, you are to creatively delight in your work.

When I was a boy, my father worked for the Radio Corporation of America as a cabinetmaker. He fashioned and polished those wooden consoles that housed the complex array of tubes and wires necessary to have good radio reception in the early days of the wireless. He was a craftsman, and though he did not get paid much for his work, he felt a tremendous sense of gratification from what he produced.

Every time he made a radio console, he put his initials on the back of it. I remember when we visited friends or relatives he would motion for me to look in the back of the console to see if his initials were there. Whenever I found them, he would nearly burst with pride. That wooden console was more than just a thing. In some mystical way he had extended himself into the production of his own product. Each console was *his*, an expression of his skills and abilities. Because he had pride in his work, he was a fulfilled man.

Today, not many workers have the privilege of finding that type of fulfilment in their work. A survey in America found that over 80 per cent of the workforce hate what they do. Thank God that wasn't true of my father.

Most of us must turn to little children to see people engrossed in their work. Have you ever watched the boys and girls working on crafts during a session of the holiday Bible club? The child who wants to make something for his mother works with a dedication and an intensity that has become all too rare in our age of shoddy workmanship. I can still see my little boy coming home from school and handing me a piece of clay that was painted green saying, 'I made it for you.' Every worker should strive for that kind of emotional payoff from his labours.

Some years ago, a friend of mine went to lecture in English literature at a certain college. He was there for three weeks when he went into the dean's office to say that he was leaving.

'I'm not coming back next week, and I thought you ought to know,' he said. The dean replied, 'If you walk out on your contract, you're not going to lecture here again. What's more, you won't lecture anywhere, if I can help it.'

After my friend left his job, his mother contacted me by phone and said I had to see him. She was sure he had gone crazy and hoped I could talk him into going back to his job.

I found my friend Charlie living in an attic apartment in Hamilton Square, New Jersey. I must admit that his apartment had style: travel posters pasted all over the walls, a good assortment of books scattered around the room, and the stereo playing a Wagnerian opera. I sat down in a beanbag chair that swallowed me up. After we had exchanged niceties I came to the point.

'What have you done?' I asked.

'I quit,' said Charlie. 'I walked out. I don't want to teach anymore. Every time I walked into that lecture room, I died a little bit.'

I could understand him. I am a teacher, and I know what it is like to go into a lecture and pour out your heart to students, to let every nerve inside you tingle with the excitement of your most profound insights. I know what it is like to passionately share the struggles of your existence, to lay your soul bare in an attempt to communicate your deepest feelings. Then, when it is all over, some student in the back of the room raises his hand and says, 'Do we have to know this stuff for the finals?'—and I die a little bit too.

It wasn't long before I realised that Charlie was not about to go back to lecturing; so I asked him what he was doing with himself these days. He said, 'I'm a postman.'

Reaching back into the value system provided by the Protestant work ethic, I said to him, 'Charlie, if you're going to be a postman, be the best postman in the world.'

He said, 'I am a *lousy* postman. Everybody else who delivers mail gets back to the post office by about two o'clock. I never get back until six.'

'What takes you so long?' I asked.

'I visit,' said Charlie. 'You'd never believe how many lonely people there are on my route who had never been visited until I became a postman. What's more, now I can't sleep at night.'

'Why can't you sleep?' I asked.

'Have you every tried to sleep after drinking fifteen cups of coffee?' was his reply.

As I sat and looked at my friend Charlie, I envied him. He was alive with the excitement that comes to a person doing something meaningful with his life. Because he moved from being a college lecturer to a postman, he has lost status. But what difference does that make? As Charlie invests himself significantly in the lives of other people, he is finding fulfilment in visiting 'orphans and widows in their distress' (Jas 1:27).

People in their early forties find it difficult to change jobs. As meaningless as many jobs are, they do offer a sense of security. W.I. Thomas, one of the founders of American sociology, analysing the basic wishes of human existence, notes that all people have a desire for security and a desire for new adventure. Thomas sees these two wishes in diametrical opposition to each other. The older we get, the more our desire for security grows and our desire for new adventure diminishes. But this does not have to be. One of the results of the new life in Christ is that 'your old men will dream dreams, your young men will see visions' (Joel 2:28).

I am always thrilled by the story of that old man Abraham, who, when he was seventy-five, decided to start life anew. The Bible says that when Abraham was called by God, he left the Ur of the Chaldees, 'not knowing where he was going' (Heb 11:8). He saw that there was more to his life that was waiting to be lived. If Abraham dared to strike out in a new direction at the age of seventy-five, why should a man of forty be afraid to do so?

A commitment to Christ can enable us to be adventurous because our need for security is gratified, not in our vocations, but in our trust in Jesus. When we commit our lives to Christ, we sense that he will be with us and support us and uphold us throughout all of life. With security we can say, 'If God is for us, who is against us?' (Rom 8:31).

Invest in family

In the attempt to create meaning out of the sense of absurdity that marks the midlife crisis, a man should take a good look at his family. In his rush to be a success, he may have overlooked the precious opportunity of having deep relationships with his wife and children. Fortunately, a man in his early forties still has time to develop the kind of family relationships that will give him a sense of success, even when all else might be making him feel that life is a failure. Too often, we become so preoccupied with our occupational roles that we let opportunities for intimacy slip away from us. Then, like Tevye in *Fiddler on the Roof* we ask, 'Where is the little girl I carried? Where is the little boy at play? I don't remember growing older—when, oh when did they?'

Often, the midlife crisis causes men to pay intense attention to those precious ones they had previously ignored. Such men discover the joy that comes from listening to their children, helping them with their problems, and wonderfully sharing their joys. These men discover, before it is too late, that there is a fantastic fulfilment in looking into their childrens' eyes when they speak, discerning not only what is being said but what is being felt and meant.

In Thornton Wilders' play, *Our Town*, a woman who has died is allowed to relive one day of her life. She chooses her twelfth birthday. Other dead people try to warn her not to do it, but she insists. As she watches herself and her family members live out that day, she is overwhelmed with despair at the way members of her family just take each other for granted. She agonises over the fact that they talk to each other without really paying attention, and she ends up crying, 'Don't they realise that they won't have each other for ever?'

If a midlife crisis shakes men out of ignoring those who are most precious to them, and causes them to give themselves to their families in an intense manner, it can then lead a man to a more meaningful life than he has ever known before.

Create community

Another option for men facing the midlife crisis is found in the creating of community. The Western family system has tended to isolate the members of the nuclear family from an extended network of blood relatives. Most people lack meaningful emotional ties with persons outside of their immediate families. In times of crisis the family is left alone, lacking a support group that could carry them through such difficult times.

In the face of this separateness, some Christian families have made decisions to establish community with other families. Sometimes, such Christian families choose to live next door to each other, so that they can share with one another in many ways. As men and women develop deep friendships, they learn that the tendency to glorify individuality at the expense of community is wrong. Jesus has created us to be members one of another, and in community we find the emotional support that can carry us through crises that might otherwise threaten our identities and concepts of self-worth.

I am suggesting that couples make a covenant with one or more other couples to remain together throughout life. I use the word *covenant* because it connotes a sacred, binding relationship. If there is a commitment to be mutually supportive, one couple will not move away from the others, even to take advantage of job opportunities that would move them up the success ladder. In order to maintain community, they are willing to stay with their friends, no matter what the vocational price, because the emotional payoff makes it worthwhile.

When several families live close by each other, it becomes possible to adopt a more inexpensive lifestyle. Instead of buying several lawnmowers, the families can buy one and share it. The same can be done with ladders, electric saws, and washing machines. Food is purchased in quantity and, hence, at reduced costs. In short, it is possible to cut the cost of living in middle-class comfort.

Surrender to Christ

In the midst of the midlife crisis, men need Jesus. A total surrender to Christ enables men to learn how to overcome the bitterness and resentment that they have harboured towards those who seem to be beating them out in the race for vocational success. They find that Christ gives them a graciousness that enables them to love their competitors and to forgive those who are ready to do them down in the competition to get ahead.

When Jesus becomes the Significant Other in men's lives, they sense how ultimately important they are. As they recognise that Jesus loves them and accepts them as they are, it becomes easier for them to love and accept themselves. In Christ, men learn that the praise of the world has no lasting significance. They learn the truth of a verse that before seemed like a cliché, 'Only one life, 'twill soon be past; only what's done for Christ will last.' they see that it is never too late to do those things that store up 'treasures in heaven, where neither moth nor rust destroys, and where thieves do not break in or steal' (Mt 6:20).

What is success?

Jesus puts emphasis on little things we do in love rather than the big things that impress other people. Our Lord described Judgement Day as a time in which some will say, 'Lord, we cast out demons, we healed people, we did many works in your name.' And Jesus will respond to those who thought that they had done great things in the eyes of the world by saying, 'Get away from me, you workers of iniquity. I never knew you' (see Matthew 7:22–23).

On Judgement Day, the Lord will reveal the value of actions that seemed relatively unimportant. He will give special recognition to those who fed the hungry, clothed the naked, visited the sick and the imprisoned, and will declare that those who have done such things are the most blessed in the kingdom of God. 'Inasmuch as ye have done it unto one of the least of these my brethren, ye have done it unto me' (see Matthew 25:35–40).

Many men have found success in taking advantage of opportunities to express love in simple ways. It is more important to express love in the little things that we can do for one another day by day than to gain fame in the eyes of the world. Christians believe that if they are faithful in these things, the Lord will make them rulers over great things. They know that those who seek to be first become last, but those who are willing to be last and servants of all will be elevated to positions of prominence in the kingdom of God.

9
Pressures on the Midlife Woman

It used to be fairly simple to work out what a woman had to do to be successful. She had to marry a decent, hardworking, successful man. The 'better' she married the more successful she would be. Her teenage years were aimed at developing those traits which would make her a desirable marital partner, because men in the rural society of bygone generations demanded far more than physical attractiveness and a pleasant personality in a potential wife. Not that good looks and a congenial manner were unimportant, but a young, aspiring farmer was also looking for someone who could cook, sew, do the housework, milk the cows, help in the planting, and perform a host of other chores that were part of a well-run farm. A young man was told that beauty was only skin deep; if he was awed by the physical attractiveness of some women, those who cared about his future would ask, 'Can she bake a cherry pie, Billy Boy, Billy Boy?'

When the urban, industrial lifestyle became predominant, many of those old role requirements were left behind. It is no longer necessary for a woman to spend many hours every day preparing food for her household, because food is industrially processed and packaged. With relative ease, the modern woman can open a can of this, a packet of that, and have an edible dinner on the table in almost no time at all. While some women delight in sewing, the majority of the clothing worn today is industrially manufactured. Since most men are not farmers, they do not need wives who can plough fields and milk cows.

The role of a woman has changed because her social situation has changed. She can no longer gain a sense of personal worth by performing those essential tasks which belonged to her in the agrarian society. Increasingly, her self-image has become dependent on her husband's opinion of her. Now, more than ever, he is the significant other who provides her with whatever sense of success she possesses. If he thinks she is a wonderful person, then she will view herself that way. But if he regards her as an unattractive, uninteresting and worthless person, in all probability, she will end up feeling like a failure.

The woman in today's world is constantly told that she has 'never had it so good'. Yet, in many ways her life has never been more difficult. Instead of the neatly defined roles prescribed for her in the past, the modern female is thrust into a complicated multiplicity of roles. She comes and goes in an endless round of exhausting activity and is frequently left without any sense of fulfilment.

The middle-class wife in today's society is expected to be a good hostess, a community volunteer, an interior decorator, a gourmet cook, a good conversationalist, an efficient purchasing agent, and a sex partner who has overcome prudish restraints.

As a mother, she is to be the social secretary for the clubs her children join, and a taxi driver who can take the children to and from their endless array of lessons, sports, and clubs. She is supposed to be a teacher's aide who can help the children in their homework, help them with projects, and maintain communications with the teachers at school. She is expected to do all these things while still keeping the house clean, washing the clothes, cooking the meals, and co-ordinating the life of the family.

It is no wonder that today's woman often feels depressed over not being able to get everything done. Her family members often take what she does for granted, giving little consideration to the time and effort expended. What is worse is that often she herself does not recognise the amount of time and energy that these taken-for-granted activities require. At the end of a day, she often feels exhausted and perplexed as she wonders, 'Where did my day go, and why wasn't I able to get more done?'

Poor preparation for motherhood

The modern woman has had little preparation for her tiring and demanding roles. She was educated in schools that gave her the same training as her husband. In college she learned to enjoy the poetry of T.S. Eliot, the paintings of Monet, and a philosophical approach to the humanities. When she married and had children, this life was suddenly interrupted when she was thrust into an endless round of chores alien to her background. She found herself spoon-feeding, changing nappies, curing rashes, and maintaining endless surveillance over the activities and bodily functions of her children.

Whatever positive things one can say about being a mother, it must be readily admitted that the middle-class female finds that becoming one does interrupt her former lifestyle. Often, the change is an abrupt cultural shock, and proves difficult to manage.

George Herbert Mead, considered by many to be America's greatest social philosopher, claimed that the games played in childhood prepare us for roles we later assume in life. He contended that children act out in play the kinds of roles that they will assume in adulthood. By this play, they become psychologically prepared for their future tasks, and to some degree, conditioned for what they will later experience.

Today's young woman lacked the kind of play activity that would have psychologically prepared her for her role. In all probability she did not play with a doll that wet its pants, cried 'Mummy', and was carted around in a toy pram. The contemporary mother probably played with a Barbie doll as a child. Barbie is a grown-up doll, a career girl in her early twenties. She has gowns and tennis outfits; she drives a convertible and has a kid sister and a boyfriend named Ken. When the childhood play habits of the modern woman cause her to identify with the footloose and fancy-free lifestyle of a career woman, she is denied some of the preparation that would make adjustment to motherhood a lot easier.

Raising children alone

It must be noted that no woman in history has been left so alone to face the responsibilities of childrearing as has the contemporary mother. In earlier times, people lived in small communities, surrounded by relatives or intimate friends. These close associates often had a wealth of experience in motherhood that they shared with the new mother. They also took care of the child from time to time, providing her with needed rest and relief. If she wanted to go to town with her husband, there was always an aunt, an in-law, a sister, or a close neighbour who would come in and mind the children. If a mother wasn't feeling well, there was usually some competent adult who would care for the child, while the mother got some rest. It is only today's mother, isolated in the modern urban world, who has had to resort to that strange curiosity called a 'baby-sitter'.

In today's world, the woman who is part of a small, mobile family unit may find herself isolated in some high-rise apartment, surrounded by strangers. When she is sick there is no one to call for help. As her husband leaves in the morning, the best that he can offer her is the promise of a telephone call during the day to see how she's doing.

Compare what the modern woman endures when raising a child to the experiences of mothers in ancient times. Specifically, compare the modern woman with Mary, the mother of Jesus. When her boy was twelve years of age, she took him to the Temple in Jerusalem for his bar mitzvah. When Mary and Joseph headed home, Jesus decided to stay behind and talk with the scribes and the scholars. He had many questions that needed answering. It wasn't until a whole day's journey had been made that Mary and Joseph realised that Jesus was not with them. Can't you just imagine Joseph saying to Mary 'I haven't seen Jesus since early morning?'

The Scriptures tell us that Mary and Joseph supposed that he had been with the others. Mary and Joseph were part of a supportive community that lovingly cared for all of its children. In the ancient world, a young mother did not raise a child by herself, but was aided in that task by a group of people who brought responsibility, experience, and knowledge to the childrearing process. It is a peculiarity of our time that a woman is left to raise children on her own.

Because so much is demanded of the modern woman, for which she is so poorly prepared, it is difficult for her to feel successful. Often she cannot handle the demands of her life, and she may become angry or depressed when everybody seems to suggest that she has it so easy.

Life in a sexist society

On top of all of this, the modern woman is subjected to the psychological consequences of living in a sexist society. When we called a society *sexist*, we are describing a social system in which females must maintain certain physical attributes and a certain personality style in order to be deemed worthwhile. In such a society, a competent female may be treated like a loser if she doesn't have a pretty face, a proper body shape, and prescribed mannerisms. Lacking these attributes, she may suffer from deep feelings of inferiority, regardless of how bright or efficient she is.

What is worse, she is expected to maintain these desirable physical traits throughout most of her life, even though it is impossible to do so. When she begins to lose her youthful looks, she may feel threatened, particularly if her husband takes an interest in younger women who seem to possess what she has lost. In her middle-aged years, she is supposed to smile benevolently as her husband drools over younger woman who parade before him on the beach, clad in bathing suits that conceal far less than they reveal. She doesn't like to admit it, but she is hurt when her husband finds their physical appearance more attractive than hers. In many ways he subtly communicates that she no longer turns him on.

It is no wonder that the suicide rate for married women over the age of thirty-five is three times higher than it is for men of the same age, and that the number of women in middle-age suffering from emotional depression far exceeds the number of men experiencing the same malady. Kate Millet explains it well when she says that men at the age of forty can be considered mature, while women at the age of forty are usually considered obsolete. This is not to suggest that there aren't attractive forty-year-old women, but only to point out that women who are attractive at that age are considered so because they don't look forty.

I have spoken at Christian women's meetings all across the USA. In almost every case, the women chairing the meeting has told me, 'There are three things that we do not talk about at our meetings: church affiliation, weight, and age.' They know all too well that when women are made conscious of their age and weight, they are simultaneously made conscious that those charms of the 'successful woman' are slipping away from them. There is no question but that society, by overemphasising the importance of physical attractiveness in women, helps to make them feel like failures when their looks are eroded by the passage of time.

Feminist arguments

Politically conservative members of the evangelical community usually fail to see the legitimacy of many of the feminist arguments. It is important for Christians to understand that, whatever their views may be on the constitutional changes sought by the feminist movement, these angry women also represent a righteous indignation against what the modern world does to women. It overtaxes them with impossible role expectations and dehumanises them by attaching so much of their personal worth to their physical appearance. While Jesus would have rejected some of the claims of the women's liberation leaders, he would have hailed their efforts to end so many of the unnecessary hurts which society inflicts upon modern women.

A careful examination of the social rebellion fostered by the feminist movement brings us to an awareness of the positions that should be supported by Christians.

1. Beauty contests. In the earliest stages of the feminist movement, some members demonstrated against beauty contests such as Miss United Kingdom and Miss America. The feminists saw the contests as something that oppressed women and diminished their sense of worth. Indeed it has surprised me that more evangelicals have not joined them in this crusade. Surely those of us who are opposed to pornography should sense that there is something wrong about a contest that has more than fifty women parading their sexual wares before the lustful eyes of millions of men. I don't want to sound like a prude, but I think the feminists are right when they say that such contests treat women as if they were pieces of meat, instead of persons.

I know that many of the Miss America contestants are Sunday school teachers and are 'Christian girls'. I know that several of them have given testimonies as to what Christ means to them. But none of that detracts from the fact that such a contest is wrong. One young woman who had been a participant in the Miss America contest heard one of my tirades against it and complained to me that the contest is more than just a display of flesh in bathing suits. I agree, but because it *does* require a display of flesh in bathing suits as part of its selection process, I believe it must be condemned.

It is amazing to me that Christians are not more irate over what goes on at televised beauty contests. Consider that each of the contestants has the various parts of her body measured and then broadcast to the world. As the Master of Ceremonies tells us that the winner is 36–26–36, women all across the country quietly compare their own measurements to this prescribed shape, and most of them come away feeling significantly inferior.

It is interesting to note that for years the Roman Catholic Church opposed its women participating. Their objections proved to have a profound basis: the Catholic hierarchy claimed that it is not the prerogative of society to define what a woman should be, but rather the prerogative of God. They argued that when society assumed the right to define for women what they should be, then that society had usurped the prerogative of God. Personally, I think the Roman Catholics were right. Why should a woman feel inferior because she fails to measure up—or down—to the measurements of a beauty queen?

In the past, part of the Miss America contest had a question time to ascertain whether a potential candidate for the crown was able to handle the difficult questions people might ask her during her hoped-for reign. In a local contest towards the end of the Vietnam War, the question was asked, 'What should be our attitude towards the men who are wearing this country's uniforms while stationed in Vietnam?'

I thought to myself, *that contestant is in trouble now. There is no way she can come out of this alive. If she answers one way, all the hawks will hate her. If she answers the other way, all the doves will hate her. She's doomed to alienate at least half of the audience.*

The contestant then responded, 'I really don't know what this war is all about. It all seems so complicated to me. I can't even figure out how we got into this war, but I think that at a time like this we should support our men wherever they are.'

I was intrigued with the answer. What this potential Miss

America said about herself was that she was stupid and uninformed. The audience loved it because it only affirmed their
idea of what an ideal women is—pretty, but not too intelligent. I thought to myself that she must be pretty smart to act
that dumb, and to play the expected role with such precision.

2. *Games women play.* This type of behaviour only encourages women to play down their intelligence in order to succeed in a society that is dominated by male chauvinists.
Women often tone down their brilliance in order to seem
more sexually attractive to men. A study done by one of my
postgraduate students showed that at the time of marriage,
the typical man and woman have pretty much the same IQ
level. However, after fifteen years of marriage, these same
women registered about ten points lower than their husbands. The women had played down their intelligence for so
long, and in so many ways, that they had finally become
what they pretended to be—not too bright.

I find that the kinds of games women play, to measure up to
the culturally prescribed criteria for their successes, are dehumanising and keep them from growing into the fullness of personhood that God intends for them. When the feminist movement attacks these destructive games, I believe the feminists
are condemning behaviour that Christ himself would oppose.

3. *Media images.* The images of females presented in the
media are often distorted. Television ads prove to be particularly objectionable for they have a history of depicting
women as people who remove dirt. I'm tired of ads where a
woman dissolves into tears because her wash isn't as clean as
her neighbour's or because she has failed to use a detergent
that would remove the ring around her husband's shirt collar.
It is no accident that the shows which are aimed at women
listeners are called soap operas, since soap is what they
usually advertise. The ads depict women as the cleaners in
society, while the ads portray men doing the responsible and
important things of life.

Fortunately, the feminist movement has made some

changes in the media. Women are being depicted more and more in roles of leadership and social responsibility. The ads are changing in order to reflect more positive roles for women. This provides encouragement for women considering jobs which in the past were reserved solely for men.

10

Women, Work, and the Feminist Movement

The feminist movement has tried to help women to establish positive identities that are not dependent on the dispositions and attitudes of their husbands. The primary means of achieving these identities are in pursuing jobs outside the home. The feminists have urged women to take positions in the professions so that their sense of worth and success can be from their own accomplishments, rather than from those of their husbands.

In former times, the primary reason for a woman working outside the home was to supplement the family income. Indeed, with inflation being what it is, a wife may have to go to work just to make ends meet. However, the women's movement suggests that careers will help women to establish positive self-identities. Such a proposal has posed a host of serious problems.

Re-entry

Many women face serious emotional strains as they struggle through what has come to be called *the re-entry problem*. They have lived for decades in a protected environment that served as a buffer against the competitive struggles of the business world. In many cases their husbands have made most of the important decisions governing the family.

The woman who decides to leave the safety of her domestic cocoon and venture out into a competitive environment may find herself extremely threatened. The feminist movement has tried to assist such women by providing assertiveness-training courses, re-entry programmes, and seminars. These initiatives are meant to help women rediscover the ability to be competitive.

Many women were employed in the early years of their marriages, but gave up their jobs when they became mothers. After several years as housewives, they find it frightening to move back into the world of business and industry.

Several years ago, my wife went through the process of applying for a job at a publishing company. She described how uncomfortable she felt as she went to be interviewed by the director of the personnel department. The sleek professionalism of this young woman made my wife feel inept and inadequate. The youthful arrogance of that personnel director may have been an attempt to cover up her own feelings of inferiority, but nevertheless, she made my wife feel so bad about herself that she came home in tears. Obviously, my wife needed strengthening if she were to go back and try again. (I should hasten to note that my wife's threatened feelings had nothing to do with her capabilities. She subsequently became an estate agent and enjoyed high earnings in the first year.)

The feminist movement has endeavoured to provide support groups made up of women who are going through the re-entry experience. These support groups enable women to encourage each other, and thereby facilitate the re-entry process.

1. *Consciousness-raising and assertiveness training*. There is no doubt in my mind but that churches should become involved in helping women to cope with today's problems. Christians are called upon to 'bear one another's burdens, and thus fulfill the law of Christ' (Gal 6:2). It seems to me that every church should form a consciousness-raising group where women can share their fears and aspirations with others who will understand and encourage them.

It is important that such groups exist within a community of believers so that women do not become seduced by anti-Christian value systems. Christian women must learn how to assert themselves without hating those individual chauvinistic males who have in the past put them down and held them back. Women need to learn how to assert themselves without becoming antagonistic towards men as a group. They must be encouraged to assert themselves without assuming the destructive aggressiveness that has too often been a part of the male vocational lifestyle.

2. *Positive image for the working mother.* Churches can further assist women who face the re-entry problem by providing teachings which give them a positive self-image. Too often, I have heard sermons which blame most of the evils of our society on the fact that a significant proportion of women are gainfully employed outside the home. Uninformed preachers too easily associate drug addiction, juvenile delinquency, teenage pregnancy, and other social problems with the fact that just over one half of British women are now in the workforce.

It is true that every child has the right to find a parent at home waiting for him or her at the end of a school day, but this parent need not be the mother. The important thing is that one of the parents should be there to greet the child, wipe the tears if it's been a bad day, provide the traditional glass of milk and biscuits, and supervise the late afternoon activities. In many cases, when both husband and wife are working, the couple may find that it is more convenient for the father to be home to greet the children.

Careful study by sociologists has pointed out that in many cases a mother employed outside the home can be a better mother. If a woman finds looking after the house to be an unfulfilling vocation, it is better for her to secure a job that offers her emotional satisfaction. Her house may not be as clean as a home maintained by a full-time housewife, but a perfectly kept house does not guarantee happy and well-adjusted children.

Otto Pollack, former professor of family studies at the University of Pennsylvania, suggests that many women who are housewives despise housework and are filled with resentment because they find themselves trapped into this role by circumstances beyond their control. They may unconsciously suppress that resentment but still it will express itself in many subtle and nonverbal ways. Children, who are better at picking up nonverbal communication signals than adults, read this resentment in their mothers and are deeply affected by it. Pollack suggests that awareness of parental resentment creates emotional disturbances in children, and results in a variety of problems that surface later in life.

According to Pollack, it is better for women to find fulfilment in work outside the home rather than to communicate repressed resentments to their children. It is more important that a child come home to a happy mother, than to an immaculately kept house.

Many churches are taking a more enlightened view on women in the workforce. They sometimes provide day-care centres and nursery schools in order to help women who have jobs in business and industry. Such private day-care centres have become increasingly necessary as a number of publicly financed centres have closed.

Recent studies indicate that 18 per cent of children in Britain are presently being reared in one-parent homes, and that there are over one million such families. Usually that parent is the mother. While we wish the situation were otherwise, the fact remains that there are thousands of mothers working outside the home who need the assistance of caring churches.

Female life expectancy and identity

A very obvious condition that emerged at the turn of the century should have stimulated us to provide training and encouragement for women who desire work other than caring for the home and family. This condition is the increasing life expectancy of women—now at seventy-six. There is, therefore, a prolonged period in their lives after the last child leaves home.

In former centuries, women married relatively early and immediately began their families. The last child left home as the woman approached fifty years of age. Since she usually did not live much longer, raising children became a primary reason for existence.

In today's world, the average women has two children, who are gone by the time she is forty-five years old. What is she to do in her last thirty years? If she thinks of herself only as a mother, these thirty years can be empty and meaningless. This is particularly true if the woman is later divorced, widowed, or separated from her husband.

Churches should be encouraging women to prepare for vocations that will provide meaning and fulfilment in those later years. Instead, many churches contend that 'a woman's place is in the home', as though this were a biblically pre-scribed principle. Actually, there is nothing in the Bible to demand that a woman be limited to the role of housewife. Biblical women ploughed fields, planted vineyards, and worked in the marketplace.

The feminists argue that a women who does not have a means of establishing identity, other than that provided by her husband, is in an emotionally precarious position. If her husband passes negative judgement on her, and she still keeps trying to carry out her traditionally assigned roles, she will find herself psychologically devastated. The feminists point out that there are few people as pathetic as women mar-ried to men who show little or no appreciation for what they are and do.

I know of one woman with five children whose husband became romantically interested in someone else. As this extramarital affair developed, he treated his wife with increasing harshness. He made disparaging remarks about the way she kept the house, complained about the quality of food at each meal, criticised the way she raised the children, and made snide remarks about her ability to perform sexually. Her whole self-concept was tied to his view of her; he alone was the significant other in her life, and when he began to define her in a negative way, she developed an increasingly poor self-image. She would go out of her way to do special things for him, and then would wait with bated breath for some positive response. Unfortunately, he had already made up his mind not to like anything she did. He eventually succeeded in turning her into a grovelling and humiliated woman who thought of herself as less than nothing.

This woman finally joined a consciousness-raising group with some feminists who helped her to realise what a fine person she really was. As she completed a college education and became a school social worker, her self-image improved significantly. Once more there was an air of joy about her. Her marriage was still a failure, but it no longer devastated her as it had before. The social adjustment of her children improved vastly, and they became more successful in their schoolwork.

What surprised me was that her pastor condemned her for not staying at home and caring for her children; he even inserted snide remarks about people like her in his sermons. Eventually, she left the church. There was no point in taking verbal abuse from someone pretending to proclaim the word of God.

The church should have provided the kind of help that the feminist group gave this woman. The church that is equipped to provide such services has the capacity to do a much better job. Unfortunately, the feminists encouraged the women to hate her husband. The church could have taught her how to become a self-realised person without hating anyone.

Mothers of rebellious children

Most mothers associate their sense of success and failure with how their children turn out. Unfortunately, there are many children who ruin their own lives or fail to measure up to their potential. In such instances, parents, and especially mothers, have a tendency to accept total blame. Then there is always some religious biddy or cantankerous church leader who self-righteously says, 'Train up a child in the way he should go' (see Proverbs 22:6).

I would be the last to suggest that parents do not exercise a very significant influence on the development of their children. However, in today's society, parents may not be the decisive influence. Sociologists point out that in the early years of schooling, the values, orientation, and lifestyles of schoolteachers may be the most important conditioning factors in the lives of many children.

Through the adolescent years, the peer group may prove to be the most important personality-forming factor. Some parents find that, in spite of all they do to bring up their children in the nurture and admonition of the Lord, their children choose friends whose lifestyles are opposed to Christian values. The parents may do their best to bring their children into contact with young people whom the parents feel would have more of a positive influence, only to find that their children are turned off by these more wholesome young people.

When a mother has done and said all that she can, and has provided the best possible example for her children, she must learn to resign herself to the fact that her children are individuals with free wills. They are quite capable of rebelling against everything that she is and advocates. Children are not as easily moulded by parents as some people think. Mothers must not condemn themselves too harshly when their children fail. They need to remember that even Mary, the mother of Jesus, had sons who were not believers in the Christ.

I predict that the next decade will witness a parents' rebellion against a society that has harshly held them accountable for their children's behaviour. The comment, 'There are no deliquent children, just delinquent parents,' is scientifically unsound and has created too many unnecessary guilt trips for too many self-effacing mothers.

Warnings about the feminist movement

There are several warnings that Christian women should heed as they face the challenges and the promises of the feminist movement.

1. Caring for the home is of value. No woman should be conned into feeling that being a housewife is a worthless and inferior vocation. While some women find that this vocation holds little emotional fulfilment, it must be noted that for many women, looking after the house and caring for children is a full-time job and provides all of the emotional gratification they could ever hope to have. While I support those who feel that their personal fulfilment requires an escape from caring for the home as a full-time job, I also want to lend encouragement to those women who find it a high and holy calling. While a woman should not feel obligated to be a full-time housewife simply by virtue of her sexual identity, she should feel free to deliberately choose this role if she believes it to be the vocation to which God has called her.

Too often feminists have overstated their cry for liberation from the traditional role expectations, leaving women who enjoy that traditionally prescribed lifestyle feeling guilty and ashamed because they don't want to be anything other than housewives. I advocate freedom for women to pursue the leading of the Holy Spirit into that vocation which God has willed for them. It is my prayer that women may enjoy that ecstasy which comes to those who feel that their life's work is important, challenging, and ordained of God.

2. The working world has its problems. Women must be warned not to fall into the same traps that have ensnared men in their vocational involvements. Too often, women in their late thirties have been inspired to re-enter the workforce, only to find out that job opportunities are scarce, and possibilities for advancement limited.

Many women have returned to college in order to gain the credentials for some prestigious position. They have worked day and night to hold house and home together while pursuing degrees, and the dream that has kept them going was that some day they would have good positions of respect and would be able to earn a good living. Unfortunately, many of these women, upon graduation, found that they were entering a job market glutted with white collar professionals. They were left angry by their failure to gain 'exciting' jobs.

Many sociologists insist that our population is overly-qualified for the kinds of jobs available. When women leave the role of housewife, they are moving into a vocational world which involves considerable risk.

3. *A family may not be supportive.* A women may have a long, difficult task in getting the other members of her family to accept her legitimate right to pursue a career that makes her feel successful. Even if they lend her verbal encouragement, they are not about to give up the easy life that her full-time attention to looking after the home has provided. They will still expect her to wash the clothes, do the dishes, clean the house, and do all the other things that she has always done. They are willing to affirm her new vocational aspirations as long as she still performs all those tasks that have been traditionally ascribed to women.

Too often a working women's husband comes home at the end of the day, throws himself into a comfortable chair, and says, 'I've had a hard day! When will supper be ready?'

She feels like screaming, *I've had a hard day too. Nobody's making dinner for me. Why don't you come in here and help?*

Husbands and children need to recognise their responsibility to become part of the housekeeping workforce when the mother goes out to get a job. They need to see that she cannot go through a role change without all of them simultaneously experiencing changes in their lifestyles. In all probability, it is going to take a lot of patient re-education to enable typical families to go through this period of transition.

4. *Vocation does not give identity.* Women need to realise that their identities should not ultimately be tied to their vocational

employment. If this is allowed to happen, women, like many men, will be threatened with a loss of identity whenever their jobs are phased out or taken from them. Only those people who achieve identity through their relationships with God are able to stand the threats and buffeting which are part of life.

When people recognise God as the ultimate Significant Other, they define their worth in terms of their relationship with him. When individuals come to love themselves as Jesus does, their sense of self-worth cannot be taken away, no matter what the world does. If they are faithful to their divine calling, a sense of success will pervade their lives, even if the world labels them failures.

11

Single People and Success

One of the chief symbols of success is a happy family. We try to convince the world that our families are more important than anything we can achieve in our workaday vocations. We like to say that money, fame, and power are of no significance unless our families are happy. We claim that our jobs are only a means to provide for the well-being of our loved ones.

While such rhetoric is lofty, the lifestyles of many people contradict their words. How else can we explain the fact that families are often neglected, as fathers work long hours to gain desired promotions? How else can we explain the countless married couples whose pursuit of success symbols leaves them too exhausted for any kind of intimate relationships? How else can we explain the many young people who, feeling that they don't measure up to their parents' expectations, fall into deep states of depression and seek escape by espousing a countercultural lifestyle?

While few people are willing to admit it openly, their personal successes are usually more important than their families. Nevertheless, an attractive spouse and bright, adorable children are necessary display objects for the successful person. William Whyte, Jr, in his book, *The Organization Man*, argues that very often parents want their children to succeed, primarily because of the way that success will reflect upon them. Whyte suggests that the father cheering for his son at the Little League game is not so much concerned about the boy's delight in hitting a home run, as he is about the way in which his son's success will reflect upon him. He looks forward to bragging about it the next time somebody asks, 'How are your kids doing?'

For a man, the family often becomes a primary means of displaying what he has achieved. How can he show the world that he has made it unless he provides a good home for his family, fine education for his children, and all the other things that the media suggest every good family should possess?

Singleness is disappointing

All of this leaves the single person in a very threatened position. If successful people are happily married, living in comfortable houses in suburbia and having beautiful children who enjoy sport, then how can the single person be successful? An individual may achieve power, gain wealth, and hold a position of prestige, but if he has failed to marry, he becomes an object of pity.

We have all noticed how parents speak with disappointment about their unmarried children. Even as they tell us about the daughter who has become a surgeon, or the son who is a prominent lawyer, we are aware that they would be happier if their children were married, even though socially less prominent. Parents make children feel guilty for not providing them with grandchildren. Few single career people can evade the fact that in spite of all they have accomplished, they have disappointed their parents in a very essential way.

Single people must constantly cope with friends who are trying to arrange marriages for them. These friends believe that this is the best way to 'help' the single individual. The thought seldom occurs to them that singleness may be a chosen way of life.

Single people are made to feel like failures in our society.

Parents are disappointed in them, and friends pity them. Society at large is embarrassed by their presence. If there is a dinner party, it is for couples. When we invite a single person, out of necessity or kindness, we usually look for a partner of the opposite sex so that the two can be more socially accept- able as a couple. Even churches are embarrassed by the pres- ence of single adults. The church is so strongly oriented to family life that we don't know what to do with these 'spare' people. The church sponsors young wives' groups and family life conferences, but very few activities for single people.

Churches here and there have attempted to correct this condition by starting single adult groups. Sometimes these gatherings provide a good social outlet. However, some groups seem to be aimed at matching people up for marriage. Many single people claim that these activities leave them depressed because of an unspoken awareness running through the group that 'We're losers.'

Single by choice

What many of us find hard to grasp is that singleness can be a chosen way of life. The apostle Paul taught that single people are more free to serve God than are those who are married. Paul made the point that the married person finds his loyalties divided between what is pleasing to God and what is neces- sary to please one's spouse. When children come, the problem becomes more complex. Every decision that a parent makes about how to live, and where to work or buy a house, is con- ditioned by how the children will be affected. Paul wrote:

> I want you to be free from concern. One who is unmarried is
> concerned about the things of the Lord, how he may please the
> Lord; but one who is married is concerned about the things of
> this world, how he may please his wife, and his interests are
> divided. And the woman who is unmarried, and the virgin, is
> concerned about the things of the Lord, that she may be holy

both in body and spirit; but one who is married is concerned about the things of the world, how she may please her husband (1 Cor 7:32–34).

I have sensed the conflict that exists in people who want to live sacrificially for God and, at the same time, want to provide the good life for their families. I too have fallen under conviction as I examine my affluent suburban lifestyle. I think I would move into an inner city situation where I could cast my lot with oppressed peoples if it were not for the fact that I am married and have children. When I think of moving into a setting that would demand sacrificial living, I have to ask, 'Would that situation be safe for my family? What kinds of schools would my children attend?' I know that many missionaries worry about the welfare of their children when trying to decide whether to serve the Lord in some backward Third World nation. Having observed what has happened to a number of missionary children, I am convinced that in many instances it would have been better if these persons had remained childless or had not gone to the field. I have seen too many young people whose psychological adjustments have been difficult because their parents reared them in remote places.

Single and ministering

For a number of years I have been associated with a particular Latin American country, where I share in a variety of missionary enterprises. When it comes to ministering to the poor and oppressed people who live in the slums or in the dilapidated villages in the countryside, I find that the Roman Catholic priests are in a better position to minister than are missionaries who go to the field married and with children.

The Protestant missionary family usually lives in a house that is considered affluent by the masses of poor people surrounding them. This difference in lifestyle can cause alienation, and prevent effective ministry. On the other hand, the priests, unencumbered by wives and children, are able to live in the midst of the slums and adopt lifestyles that make people aware that these servants of God are one with them in every way. I am not suggesting that this is what all priests do, but only that they are more able to do this than are missionaries who have to care for families.

Roman Catholicism has always glorified the choice of singleness, if that choice is made in order to serve Christ and other people. It is about time for Protestant Christians to recognise that the Bible does teach singleness as the preferred state. Paul admonished Christians to stay single if at all possible:

> I wish that all men were as I am. But each man has his own gift from God; one has this gift, another has that. Now to the unmarried and the widows I say: It is good for them to stay unmarried, as I am. But if they cannot control themselves, they should marry, for it is better to marry than to burn with passion (1 Cor 7:7–9, NIV).

I have heard theologians and biblical scholars try to give reasons why, in spite of these verses, marriage is the preferred state for the believer. I personally feel that such theologies are rationalisations evading an obvious biblical truth. The ideal lifestyle for Christians was set by One who was single.

In the light of this, people ask me, 'Then why are you married?' I am married because I need to be. Life without my wife would be unthinkable. And that is the point that the apostle Paul was trying to make: there are some people who have to be married, but if you are going to serve Jesus in difficult places, it is better to be single. Protestant Christianity should provide special praise for those who choose to remain single in order to serve Christ more effectively. Instead of labelling them as failures, as we subtly do, we should be affirming these single people as the most successful followers of Christ.

Single and miserable

There are people who are single by no choice of their own. They would like to be married, and they feel very frustrated because they have failed to meet a member of the opposite sex who would be a desirable marriage partner. I know Christians who could have married had they been willing to settle for partners who did not share their Christian convictions. But they decided to adhere to the admonition of Scripture not to be unequally joined to nonbelievers (see 2 Corinthians 6:14).

Even so, these people feel left out because other Christians have found partners. They wonder why they have not been as fortunate, and may repress envy as they view their married friends.

Some single adults go through periods of seriously questioning their own worth as persons, asking 'What's wrong with me? Why don't people find me attractive? Why am I such a loser?'

Such questioning can immobilise them, leaving them in a state of depression. They are faced with the ugly reality that our society specialises in superficiality. The world of films and advertising has glorified glamour, and the unglamourous people get left out of the marriage market. A statement such as, 'Looks aren't everything.' does not alleviate pain for people who are suffering rejection because they lack the face or figure to 'turn on' members of the opposite sex.

Is it a source of comfort to recognise that Jesus looks for an inner beauty that is not conditioned by the culturally prescribed criteria for attractiveness? One of my good friends, who is a single female, cried, 'I find little comfort in knowing that Jesus thinks I'm beautiful, when none of the men I like thinks that I am.'

I wish there were words I could say that would leave her feeling better. There are men with enough sense to see the beauty of her heart, and I hope and pray that she meets one of them.

Some people perceive their singleness as the failure of God. I have been asked, 'Why did God let me down like this? Why didn't he plan for me to have a husband? If marriages are arranged in heaven, why didn't he arrange one for me?'

I do not presume to know the mind of God, nor am I able to grasp how his will is worked out in the world. I do not want to point out that God does not manipulate people as though they were robots. He does not make the 'right' person marry the 'right' person. Whatever God may have planned before the foundation of the world is way beyond my knowledge. I do know that what he has planned for us is not always what happens to us.

The apostle Paul did not speak of husband/wife selection as if it were the result of some celestial mating computer. There is almost a casualness in the way he described how an individual should take a marital partner. Paul seems to be saying that you get married because you like somebody and it seems right to marry that person. I think that we have come to blame too many things on God. Being left in the marriage market should not be one of them.

Single and worthy

Those who have not chosen singleness, but find themselves unmarried, can pursue a number of courses of action to enhance their feelings of worth. Many single people compensate for not being married by achieving greater success in their vocational sphere. The career teacher may be able to devote more time and attention to students than a married teacher could. The single scholar may be able to achieve successes in research that will more than compensate for not marrying. Indeed, many people have seized upon their singleness and made it an asset instead of a liability.

Singles in community

A very interesting and hopeful lifestyle for single people has begun to emerge—Christian community. One Presbyterian church in the part of Pennsylvania were I live has encouraged groups of single people to buy houses and live together as families. Six women following the advice of the pastor have established such a home. In another house four men have adopted the same plan. These people are finding that their loneliness is dispelled. They have the emotional support of people who are committed to them, and they never lack partners with whom they can share social life. I have watched these people enjoy companionship for holidays. I think the option they have chosen is not only good but also one that God would desire.

The individuality that forces us to live alone is a dimension of our culture and not an outgrowth of biblical teaching. I believe the Christian life was meant to be lived in community, and that in establishing community, these single people are more fully approximating God's will. I am not saying that you cannot be a Christian and live alone, but I am saying that as a Christian you should not *want* to live alone. Christianity is a lifestyle of sharing and self-giving. Many Christians are finding that community living is one of the best ways to work out these imperatives.

As I talk to many single people, I find that one of their most common fears is facing the later years of their lives alone. Singles who develop a community in which there is deep binding commitment are delivered from that anxiety.

Another advantage of living in community is that it can provide a wholesome environment for the adoption of children. The law does not necessitate marriage as a precondition for adoption, either in Britain or most states in the USA. The six women I mentioned have adopted three children, and are providing a good and happy home for them. The women are overjoyed and the children are blooming.

Most touching is that one of the adopted children is physically handicapped. These six women working together have provided a better home for him than could have been given by a married couple. The extra work involved in rearing this handicapped little boy is shared by the women, and none of them is overburdened by the responsibility. The parents of the six women treat the adopted children as grandchildren. The singleness of these women has not deterred them from finding happiness, or feeling that their lives are successful.

Single and sexual

As we try to understand what single people face as they live in a world that tends to view singleness as a personal failure, we need to consider the subject of sexuality as it relates to single people.

James H.S. Bossard, my sociology professor at the University of Pennsylvania, called this 'the age of the pure orgasm'. By that he meant that people have been conned into believing they can never be fulfilled as persons unless they have an active sex life. Indeed, some followers of Masters and Johnson suggest that pleasurable intercourse is a prerequisite for feeling fulfilled as a human being.

I have read several Christian writers who approve of masturbation as a means for single people to gain a sense of sexual fulfilment. These writers have suggested that such behaviour is not contrary to the will of God and that single Christians should overcome the guilt which they have for so long associated with the practice.

From a sociological point of view, certain things cause us to question this practice. Social scientists have learned that most people fantasise while they are masturbating. They tend to imagine themselves having intercourse with attractive persons. One woman, while masturbating, usually pretended that she was having intercourse with a former fiancé now married to another woman. She wanted to know if what she was doing was a form of adultery. She was disturbed about the teachings of Jesus who said: 'You have heard that it was said, 'Do not commit adultery.' But I tell you that anyone who looks at a woman lustfully has already committed adultery with her in his heart' (Mt 5:27, NIV).

Another fact that some social scientists now understand is that the craving for orgasm declines in people who cease having them. The less often an individual has an orgasm, the less often he craves one. The reverse is also true. The more an individual engages in activity that leads to orgasm, the more intensified the desire becomes.

The single person who is not engaging in sexual activity that leads to orgasm in all probability will not live with a high level of frustration.

Divorce

Divorce is a failure. A couple experiencing divorce realises that what they had hoped for at the time of their marriage has not come true.

An individual involved in a divorce will often feel guilty and go through intense self-evaluation trying to determine his responsibility for what happened. Anyone looking for a reason to blame himself for a broken marriage undoubtedly will find it. In any marriage, the participants do and say things which hurt the relationship. Should the marriage fail, the guilt associated with that behaviour can become inordinate.

1. *Self-condemnation*. There are some people, usually out of Christian backgrounds, who have an unhealthy tendency towards self-condemnation. They have been brought up not to find fault with others when anything goes wrong, but always to ask, 'How did I fail? What did I do wrong?'

A divorce encourages the individual who is overly self-condemning to conclude that he or she is totally responsible for what happened and to label himself or herself a failure. That person's self-esteem drops to such an unparalleled nadir that it becomes difficult to overcome feelings of worthlessness.

If the divorced person has been abandoned or rejected by the former partner, feelings of worthlessness are even more intensified. Such an individual may feel completely unlovable and unworthy of anyone's attention or concern. One woman I know, whose husband deserted her and their three children in order to pursue a woman who worked in his office, made it clear to me that she thought the divorce was all her fault. 'After all,' she said, 'you wouldn't expect him to stay with somebody as unattractive as I am. I'm so ordinary that it's no wonder he left me.'

2. *Childrearing*. The divorced person left with children to raise only has the problem compounded. Coming out of a marriage that failed, the solitary parent is usually threatened with the fear of also failing in childrearing. Raising children is difficult enough, even when each parent has the support of a sympathetic partner; raising children alone may seem like an almost impossible task.

Very often a divorced mother lacks the financial means to run a successful home because the court has ordered child maintenance payments which are too limited, or because the payments ordered rarely appear. It is hard to feel like anything but a failure when she lacks the means to provide an adequate lifestyle for her children. Furthermore, trying to be both mother and father can leave the individual totally exhausted and consequently, depressed. Depression causes an even greater sense of failure and distorts evaluations of personal worth.

Just for the record, sociological studies conclusively show that children who are raised by a divorced parent have just as good a chance of achieving a healthy emotional and psychological adjustment as a child reared in an intact family. This is good news especially since recent government statistics indicate that 18 per cent of Britain's children are raised in single-parent homes, the majority of which are created by divorce or separation. These statistics should convince the divorced parent that his children are not unusual because they are being raised by one parent.

3. *The Church*. The victims of unsuccessful marriages are broken people who need to be put back together again by the church. However, the church, instead of providing part of the solution for these people, often becomes part of the problem. Sometimes church members enhance the guilt feelings felt by the divorced people in their congregations. They may do this by acting as though the divorced persons should have stayed with their partners regardless of the consequences, and in spite of the fact that their partners may not have wanted them. These members make such statements as, 'She should have stayed with him for the sake of the children, if for no other reason.'

Studies indicate, to the contrary, that being raised by a single divorced parent gives a child a much greater chance of achieving emotional and psychological well-being than if that child is raised in what some social scientists call 'an empty shell marriage'.

The Bible does not prohibit divorce. The Scriptures recognise that a marriage can become intolerable.

> To the married, I give this command (not I, but the Lord): A wife must not separate from her husband. But if she does, she must remain unmarried or else be reconciled to her husband. And a husband must not divorce his wife (1 Cor 7:10–11, NIV).

Some scholars suggest that even the apostle Paul may have suffered a divorce. We know he was married because he was a member of the Jewish Sanhedrin, and marriage was a pre-requisite for membership in that august body. These scholars pose that after his conversion, Paul and his wife may have separated because she could not adhere to his new lifestyle and belief. While this is speculation, some people wonder if an unhappy marriage could be part of the reason Paul extolled singleness as a preferred state.

4. *Remarriage*. The probability that a divorced person will

remarry is relatively high. Divorced people are more likely to get married than are single people of the same age. Increasingly, the church is having to deal with divorced and remarried persons in its membership, recognising that such persons are no longer isolated curiosities, but a common presence.

The problem that most Christians have with the divorce issue stems from the explicit teachings of Jesus on the subject:

Therefore what God has joined together, let not man separate.' When the disciples asked Jesus about this, he answered, 'Anyone who divorces his wife, except for marital unfaithfulness, and marries another woman commits adultery' (Mt 19:6,9, NIV).

It is hard to get around these verses if one holds to the Bible as being inspired by the Holy Spirit. And it is easy to see why so many Christians categorically condemn divorced people who have remarried.

On the more liberal side of the issue, there are many who contend that Christians should be gracious towards the divorced and the remarried. They argue that Jesus is the Lord of the second chance, a Saviour who offers to people both forgiveness for their mistakes and an opportunity to start over again.

There are those who argue that social practices like divorce and remarriage must be understood in the light of the times in which they were established. In the ancient world a divorced woman was usually abandoned with no means of support. Often she had to resort to prostitution to survive. Divorce left her without dignity and rights, so that no Christian would ever reduce his marital partner to such a dehumanised condition. Since the times and conditions have changed, the argument goes, so should our pronouncements on divorce.

Others say that divorce is only a legal arrangement that permits the individual to take another partner but does not absolve the partner from responsibility for the well-being of his or her former spouse, until death parts them. In short, while the individual may be separated or divorced from the original partner, there is still a responsibility to see to it that the person has his or her economic needs met and is the recipient of concern until the end of life. The claim is made that the individual who fulfils these responsibilities has upheld the basic intent of Jesus' teachings.

I do not believe the problem can be resolved so simply. But I have learned to accept my divorced and remarried friends as brothers and sisters in Christ. While I do not encourage remarriage, I try not to be judgmental towards these people.

5. *Principled and gracious.* I think the church is obligated to accept the difficult challenge of upholding a principle, on the one hand, and being gracious to the violators, on the other. This is extremely difficult, because graciousness to violators can easily be interpreted as laxity concerning the principle. The church must stand opposed to divorce and remarriage, yet remain accepting and open towards those who violate the principle.

Jesus demonstrated this balance when the Pharisees brought to him a woman 'caught in the very act' of adultery. The teachings of Scripture called for the stoning to death of a woman caught in adultery. Rather than being judgmental, Jesus showed grace to the woman, forgave her, and gave her a new start in life (see John 8:1–11).

No one could ever accuse Jesus of being lax concerning biblical principles. He stood on trial before Pilate, as One who had not violated the Law in any way, and in whom no one could find any fault. But this same Jesus who came to fulfil the Law, not to destroy it, constantly showed grace to those who had failed to uphold the Law and needed a new beginning. When he met Zaccheus, he did not condemn, but rather showed loving acceptance of a man whose lifestyle would have been judged severely by the religious legalists of his day.

Widowhood

The death of a partner can deal a serious blow to the survivor's will to live. What does it matter if you have money, power, and social respect if the most important human being in your life is snatched from you? Many people are able to define themselves as successful because their partner, as significant others in their lives, have made them feel successful in spite of the discouragement and buffeting encountered in the world. In more cases than we can imagine, the death of a marital partner leaves an individual without the one person who has made him or her feel significant and successful.

The loss of a partner is particularly hard for a woman whose position in society was gained through marriage. For such a woman, the husband's death is not only the loss of a partner, but also a major threat to her own social status.

I know of one pastor's wife who experienced a complete breakdown after her husband died. Her whole identity had been wrapped up in her claim that she was married to the most prominent religious leader in the community. Being the minister's wife had made her a leader of several organisations in the church. The community had viewed her and her husband as a team in ministry, and rightly so. She had played the organ, led the choir, was an officer in the women's group, and had run the junior youth fellowship. Suddenly, her husband died of a heart attack. Not only did this woman lose her husband but also her social identity as well.

She tried to remain a member of the church, but this proved to be a problem to everyone. The wife of the new pastor quickly replaced her in many of those positions which had been such a part of her life. The new pastor, feeling nervous about having his predecessor's wife as the director of music, manoeuvred her out of that position as quickly as possible. The widow went into a depression that required psychiatric treatment. Her depression was the result of loss, not only of her dear husband but also of the success symbols that were associated with her role as his wife.

Persons facing this kind of a loss find it almost impossible to overcome the pain of the situation without the help of others. A church fellowship must recognise responsibility to provide a new and positive self-image to the widow and, in many cases, to the widower. Persons who have suffered the loss of partners need to feel an identity and significance all their own and know that their worth stands apart from the status of their former partners. It is the task of the church to discover their personal gifts and encourage them to use these gifts in the service for others. Furthermore, the church should pour out appreciation to these people for what they do and who they are.

When I was a young pastor, one of my greatest failings was in not pronouncing publicly my gratitude for the many things that elderly widows and widowers did to serve the church. Every congregation should be bending over backwards to make these people feel appreciated.

Churches that are trying to be true to their calling should heed the words of the apostle James: 'This is pure and undefiled religion in the sight of our God and Father, to visit orphans and widows in their distress, and to keep oneself unstained by the world' (Jas 1:27).

The organisation Cruse offers one-to-one counselling of individuals who have been bereaved and social support to the newly bereaved. But the organisation does not give long-term support—it believes that after support has been given, people who have been bereaved should again mix with all types of people and live as normally as possible.

Too often, the only way the church knows to alleviate the loneliness of those who have lost their husband or wife is to marry them off to some new partners. The tendency to play matchmaker is more intense when the widows or widowers are relatively young. But often such good intentions can result in hurting people even more. The efforts are interpreted as evidence that they cannot arrange their own lives or are incapable of attracting members of the opposite sex on their own.

Widowed persons frequently have no desire to enter into new marriages. While their marriages were happy, some widows and widowers don't feel they have the time and energy to go through the whole adjustment process again. It would be better if the church concentrated on helping these people to gain positive identities and to sense worthwhile accomplishments that are explicitly their own.

The death of a partner leaves the widow or widower feeling that there was so much more that could have been done for the deceased. People in this situation often feel that they failed to be the marital partner they could have been. They remember all the things that they said and did which cannot be erased. They are even more aware of what they failed to say or do. With such feelings of failure, these individuals need assurance that God forgives and forgets.

One of the most comforting doctrines of Scripture is the good news that God has blotted out our sins and remembers them no more. Those who are with him take on his character; loved ones now with the Lord can forget the wrongs that happened in this world. I believe that in the afterlife, the negative things that transpired between marital partners will not be remembered.

12

The Throwaway People

Growing old in Western society does not bring the honour and respect that it did in ancient cultures. Ours is a youth-oriented society, and when youth is lost, so is the glamour of living. Consequently, it is no wonder that the cosmetic industry earns millions of pounds each year producing the means by which the aging process can be concealed.

What is true in Britain is true for all industrial societies. Young people are preferred because they are more adaptable to the rapid changes of the modern world. In preindustrial societies, the elderly were respected because they had mastered craft skills which were the basics of economic production. The young looked with awe towards the elderly who knew how to do with perfection those things which the young wanted to learn.

Retirement

In today's society, old age usually means retirement. For some this may be a welcome period of life, but for most people, it is covertly dreaded. This is particularly true for men whose identities are so wrapped up with their jobs that when they retire, they often lose the clear definition of who they are. People who had positions of social prestige, and enjoyed the deference granted by employees under them, find these symbols of success suddenly gone.

Many retired people don't know what to do with the vast amount of time suddenly on their hands. Always before, life had been intensely organised, every minute of the day full of important tasks that gave a sense of significance. For many men, the fact that they had no time for 'trivialities' convinced them that they were people of importance. With retirement, all of that changes, and for many men this free time becomes an unbearable burden.

In my own counselling experience, many elderly women have come to me complaining about their retired husbands who follow them around all day. The husbands just don't know what to do with themselves. These women tell me how their once prestigious partners have been reduced to pathetic personalities, simply because they are lost in this new world of leisure time. There is a rising divorce rate among retired people, and one of the causes cited is that wives cannot cope with husbands who expect to be constantly entertained. What some of these wives do not admit is that they have lost respect for their husbands, now that they no longer have prestigious positions.

Women seem to be able to handle the retirement years more easily. This is particularly true for the middle- and upper-middle-class women who find that the retirement of their husbands does not significantly alter their lifestyles. After the children are raised, many of these women spend as many as twenty-five years keeping their homes tidy, belonging to tennis clubs, attending church activities, and watching television. The retirement of their husbands does not change most of that. Consequently, there is no traumatic transition as they move into the twilight years.

Economic identity of the elderly

One of the most depressing aspects of old age is that economic factors often cause the elderly to see themselves as worthless and insignificant. Feelings of failure are common among old people confined to small, dilapidated homes. Inflation lessens the value of their fixed income and diminishes the significance of their savings. People who were once proud of their independence often find themselves dependent on the state for survival. Their grown-up children with their own families to care for, often have little left to maintain elderly parents in the manner to which they had been accustomed. Poor elderly people often see themselves as burdens to family and society and simply wait for death. In a society that puts a high premium on success, these people see themselves as failures. They live out their lives feeling that they have come to nothing.

It is no wonder that my wife urges me to work out ways for us to be wealthy in our old age. She has observed that the elderly who are rich are still respected, taken places, and treated with care and thoughtfulness by their children and relatives. There may be more truth to her observations than I am willing to admit. In many cases, care by others in the waning years of life is dependent upon how much money the elderly person has to will to those others at death.

Retirement homes

Retirement homes sometimes have disastrous effects on the identity of the elderly. This is not an indictment of all retirement homes; for some, particularly those which are church related, effectively enhance the personal worth of their residents, and enable them to maintain a sense of significance throughout life. However, it is obvious that many establishments for the elderly strip them of dignity and leave them as vegetating creatures who wonder why death doesn't come sooner.

I recall, as a young pastor, visiting an elderly member of my congregation who was residing in a country home for the aged. When I signed in at the reception desk, I noticed from the card that the last time this woman had been visited by anyone was eighteen months ago. In the ward, I made my way down an aisle that neatly separated twenty beds. The room was immaculately clean, and the bed-linen had been changed that morning. Ample food was provided to the patients and yet there was a sterileness about the ward that immediately depressed me. While the people were being cared for physically, they seemed to be stripped of person-hood. In bed after bed were elderly women with glazed looks on their faces. They had handled the absurdity of their plight by emotionally detaching themselves from their environment and travelling via imagination to a time and place when things were better.

I finally found the woman I was seeking, introduced myself, and tried to make a pleasant conversation. As the lunch hour approached, a nurse came in to feed the patients. She went to the first bed, prised open the mouth of the elderly occupant, shoved a spoonful in her mouth and yelled, 'Swallow it!'

She repeated the process about five times before I mustered the courage to get up from where I was sitting, go over to her, and boldly ask, 'Do you have to do it that way?'

She stood up straight, looked down at me and said, 'You're a minister, aren't you?'

As a young pastor I prided myself on looking like a 'nor-mal' person. Since people were usually shocked to discover that I was a clergyman, I was disappointed at being so easily recognised, and asked, 'How did you know?'

She said, 'Your kind is always coming in here complaining about the things I do. Mister, I have forty patients to feed in an hour. I wish I could be gentle, but the limitation on my time forces me to do things in a very unpleasant manner. If you're concerned about the way these women eat, why don't you get the women's group of your church to spend one day a week giving them lunch? It will probably beat what they usually do with their time.'

The surprising thing was that when I made that recommendation to the group, the women rejected it. It seemed as though they were more willing to prepare bandages for the suffering people in Africa than to feed the elderly who lived down the street. Why is it that we always find it so much easier to express concern from a distance?

Our society cannot content itself by providing 'adequate' care for the elderly in such conditions. The psychological damage experienced in such settings must be a subject for our concern.

Responses to aging

We should all be aware of two facts. First, as the younger people who are voting and making the decisions that determine the fate of the elderly, we are creating the conditions in which we ourselves must eventually live. And second, Jesus was particularly concerned about the plight of the elderly and often measured commitment to God by the way people treated the elderly widows. I too believe that the measure of our Christian love can be seen in the way in which we treat the elderly.

The responses of people to the threats of old age have been varied. Many, upon retirement, have moved to areas of the country where the scenery is more attractive, and the climate milder. For instance, the South coast of England has become famous as a residence for senior citizens. After retirement, an elderly couple can sometimes find excitement and challenge by moving to a new location and 'starting life over again'. The new setting means new friends, a new church, a new house, and a new lifestyle. These challenges can occupy time and give the elderly significant things to do. What is more, they have excuses for making trips back home to visit former friends and relatives and report on their happy circumstances in retirement. But this option is available only to those who have a good income.

Some of the elderly have opted for staying put on their old

familiar territory. They often find an exciting lifestyle in the activities of a local senior citizens club. Communities all across the country have these clubs that sponsor excursions, visits to places of interest, socials, and classes for the elderly.

It is sad when retired people deprive themselves of the enjoyment of such activities simply because they are afraid of the social labels that they think are on people who belong to such organisations. Wanting to perpetuate the myth that they are not old, they refuse to join clubs for the elderly.

The church and the elderly

Every church should be either a supporter or sponsor of group activities for senior citizens. Even small churches can enter into co-operative relationships with other churches or community organisations in order to make sure that retired people enjoy the rich, recreational life to which they are entitled.

Churches have a responsibility to honour the elderly who have served them. There should be special recognition dinners, participation in the worship services, and other special ways to let the elderly know the importance of their contributions.

The congregation should not wait until its elderly members die before fellowship halls, Sunday school rooms, or organs are dedicated in their honour. The church can be the significant other for the elderly, reflecting to them such a sense of status that they will feel they have lived successfully, even as life winds down.

Some churches have put retired people to work in significant ways. The elderly make excellent associate pastors, and many congregations have found their ministry enriched by having retired members take on the job of ministry of visitation-evangelism. Still other churches have called upon retired members to serve as administrators, thus enhancing the efficiency of the churches' programmes. Some retired people have become lay preachers for small congregations that could never afford to pay their pastors. In most cases, these retired people work without a salary to make possible ministries which could never be funded by existing church budgets.

Elderly people have a vast array of professional skills which are desperately needed in developing nations. Churches would do well to encourage some of their retired members to consider placement overseas. Such positions offer excellent opportunities for the missionary enterprise. Retired people serving in Third World countries can ally themselves with indigenous churches and contribute to the ministry of Christ. Such activities can give retired people a greater sense of significance and success than they ever achieved in their pre-retirement years.

A final word about value

Ultimately, the church speaks the final word about the value of life. When we face death, much of what we have deemed significant in life appears meaningless. Death forces us to view the worthlessness of so many things that we have worked hard to achieve. We often try to escape its reality by hyperactivity, in the hope that this will protect us against 'morbid' reflection. Nevertheless, in the waning years of life, we sense ourselves moving inexorably towards that final threat to the wealth, power, and prestige that we have worked so hard to achieve. One German philosopher writes, 'We make so much noise on New Year's Eve because we are trying to drown out the macabre sound of grass growing over our own graves.'

The gospel has good news: what we have attempted to do for Christ and his kingdom will not be lost. We are informed by the apostle Paul that the good work which Christ has begun in us will continue until the day of his coming (see Philippians 1:6). We need to know that our efforts for Christ and his kingdom will not evaporate. The message of God seems to be that it is better to fail in a cause that will ultimately win than to win in a cause that will ultimately fail.

Christians *can* approach death knowing that they have been part of a movement which will triumph in history. Whatever their involvement in the work of God, they will receive their reward. Even those who look upon their labours as insignificant are informed that they shall stand before the ultimate Judge and be told, 'Well done, good and faithful servant! You have been faithful with a few things; I will put you in charge of many things' (Mt 25:21, NIV).

What does death mean for people who do not feel they have served Jesus in any significant way? I can only suggest that Jesus himself says that many will be surprised on the Day of Judgement as to how much they did accomplish; they fed the hungry, clothed the naked, visited the sick, and ministered to those who were in prison. Jesus will tell them that what they did for the least of the brethren, they did for the Lord himself (see Matthew 25:34–40).

What does death mean for those who are sure they have failed to serve Christ at all? I believe that there will be service that we can render to the Lord after we go to be with him because service is the ultimate form of worship.

To those who approach death with a feeling of failure, I say that there is endless eternity in which you can succeed for Jesus. All that he asks is that you recognise your salvation as a gift which results from his grace, and is not dependent upon your own achievements. What greater sense of success can you hope for than the awareness that you have, in eternity, an everlasting opportunity to fulfil God's plans for you?

13
A Theology of Success

A good friend once asked me, 'Isn't it true that the person who lives in accord with the will of God and patterns his life after the teachings of Scripture can expect to live a successful life?'

My answer was, 'Yes, but I am not sure that the kind of success which will be delivered is exactly what you have in mind.'

Too many people believe that faith in God and adherence to his laws will deliver wealth, power, and status. They have heard sermons or read books which suggest that faith in God and obedience to his word guarantee social success. They imagine that they will move up the socioeconomic ladder by virtue of their goodness. They assume that when the apostle Paul promises that God will 'do exceedingly abundantly beyond all that we ask or think, according to the power that works in us' (Eph 3:20), he means believers will prosper in miraculous ways and lack for nothing in the way of this world's goods.

Will Herberg, a contemporary Jewish social philosopher who has observed the American way of life, claims that they have 'faith in faith'. They think believing in God assures them of economic prosperity and personal achievement. He may be right. But this kind of 'faith' makes God a means to our own personal ends and declares that he is there to help us to achieve things which society tells us are important.

The eternal God does not exist to serve our ends. He is not an instrument for the fulfilment of our wishes. We exist to serve him. We are called to be instruments of his will.

Prayer as magic

Many sociologists differentiate religion from magic by pointing out that in religion people submit themselves to the will of a high power; in magic, people try to manipulate a higher power to get things for themselves. Many people who think they have true religion transform the Christian faith into a primitive form of magic, treating God as though he were the genie of the magic lamp. Prayer becomes a litany for manipulating God into delivering what the petitioners want. Jesus' name becomes a magical incantation that must be blasphemously uttered at the end of the prayer if God is to deliver the desired results. For many, prayer reflects the kind of immaturity that my little boy expressed one evening when he came into our living room and said, 'Before I go to bed, I'm going to pray. Does anybody want anything?'

A certain success

I believe that the Christian lifestyle does deliver success to people, but not the kind of success that is understood by society. Jesus never promised wealth, power, and prestige to those who would follow him. He warned that while foxes had holes and birds had nests, the disciples were following One who would not have a place to lay his head (Mt 8:20). He was scorned and rejected by the people of this world. Then as now, the social establishment would crucify him. Jesus warned his followers that what happened to him would happen to them.

> If the world hates you, keep in mind that it hated me first. If you belonged to the world, it would love you as its own. As it

is, you do not belong to the world, but I have chosen you out of the world. That is why the world hates you. Remember the words I spoke to you: 'No servant is greater than his master.' If they persecuted me, they will persecute you also. If they obeyed my teaching, they will obey yours also. They will treat you this way because of my name, for they do not know the One who sent me (Jn 15:18–21, NIV).

There is truth in the saying, 'When Jesus calls a man, he bids him come and die.'

Perhaps a trip through some of the poor Third World countries would shock Christians who have a Pollyana theology. They would see a contemporary witness to the fact that godly people do not necessarily get rich. In the back hills of Haiti, I have observed Christians rising at five in the morning to pray and sing praises to God before they begin their work. The devotion of these people to Christ and their faithful obedience to his word is an inspiration. Yet, despite their love for Christ and willingness to do his will, these people suffer from terrible poverty and privation. Haitian Christians experience real joy, but it is not based on economics. Life for them *is* successful, but they can't measure that success in status symbols.

Life after death

The belief that godly people will become economically prosperous and socially honoured emerges from a misinterpretation of ancient Orthodox Judaism. The Old Testament Jews had no clear concept of life after death. Many have suggested that Judaism was and is the most existential of all religions, with the rewards of a godly life being experienced in this world in the lifetime of the true believer.

At the time of Christ, the Sadducees—the most orthodox of Jews—held no belief in the afterlife, and mocked Jesus because he did. In an intriguing confrontation, they tried to trap him by making belief in the life after death seem ridiculous. After telling a story of seven brothers who had all been married to the same woman, the Sadducees asked:

> 'At the resurrection, whose wife will she be of the seven, since all of them were married to her? Jesus replied, 'You are in error because you do not know the Scriptures or the power of God. At the resurrection people will neither marry nor be given in marriage; they will be like the angels in heaven. But about the resurrection of the dead—have you not read what God said to you, "I am the God of Abraham, the God of Isaac, and the God of Jacob"? He is not the God of the dead but of the living' (Mt 22:28–32, NIV).

Jesus clearly teaches a life after death, and it is that doctrine which forces us into a new and deeper understanding of success and failure. Because this life is brief when compared with eternity, success and failure cannot be understood within the context of space and time. Within human history, those who succeed may not be those who ultimately know success. This is clear in that famous parable which Jesus gives us concerning the rich man and Lazarus.

> There was a rich man who was dressed in purple and fine linen and lived in luxury every day. At his gate was laid a beggar named Lazarus, covered with sores and longing to eat what fell from the rich man's table. Even the dogs came and licked his sores. The time came when the beggar died and the angels carried him to Abraham's side. The rich man also died and was buried. In hell, where he was in torment, he looked up and saw Abraham far away, with Lazarus by his side. So he called to him, 'Father Abraham, have pity on me and send Lazarus to dip the tip of his finger in water and cool my tongue, because I am in agony' in this fire.' But Abraham replied, 'Son, remember that in your lifetime you received good things, while Lazarus received bad things, but now he is comforted here and you are in agony' (Lk 16:19–26, NIV).

The New Testament makes it clear that it may be hard to perceive the rewards of a godly life this side of heaven, but beyond the grave the 'first will be last; and the last, first' (Mt 19:30). Those who are first in status here may not be so honoured on the other side of the grave. The Orthodox Judaism of the Sadducees—which I believe to be a misinterpretation of the Old Testament—taught that the godly would be prestigious, powerful, and wealthy in this world. However, those who believe in the resurrection and the life everlasting do not find themselves boxed in with such limitations. We Christians believe that for those who are in Christ there is a blessedness which transcends capitalistic value systems, and more than compensates for whatever privations and offences we may suffer in this life. We, with the apostle Paul, can say: 'I consider that our present sufferings are not worth comparing with the glory that will be revealed in us' (Rom 8:18, NIV).

Evidence of election

The misconception that faith in God and obedience to his Law automatically deliver wealth, power, and prestige has been derived not only from the Judaism of the Sadduccees, but also from some versions of Protestantism. Max Weber, in his classic sociological work, *The Protestant Ethic and the Spirit of Capitalism*, contends that certain Protestants, particularly those in the Calvinistic traditions, have twisted Reformed theology in order to make wealth the evidence of divine election. Through careful historical analysis, Weber points out that there were some Calvinists who wanted concrete evidence that God had chosen them to be saved. The doctrine of predestination declared that God had already decided who would be saved and who would be lost. However, these Calvinists still wondered what the evidences or signs of divine election might be. How would the saved know if they were saved?

Many Christians answered that the saved would know of their election because they would economically prosper. Thus, prosperity became the evidence of a right relationship with God. Weber is not saying that Calvin actually propagated this idea; but it was commonly circulated within the Calvinist tradition. And in this group were the Puritans, who provided some of the character of our culture.

Weber argues that as a result of the Protestant work ethic, people have endeavoured to accumulate wealth as a symbol of salvation. The clearest evidence of this is the materialism of America, which has resulted from a belief system that makes economic success evidence of one's personal worth and standing with God. Often without knowing why, people in this tradition work incessantly to accumulate as much money as possible. Subconsciously, they want to assure themselves that they are God's elite. Even though they have more than enough money to live comfortably, they work night and day. For them wealth has a symbolic value that they may not fully understand: it not only provides them with comfort, but also with psychological security. Economic success assures them that they are God's people.

Arrogant unconcern

Such a belief system can create an arrogance in the wealthy, causing them to look upon the less fortunate with contempt. We may have heard religious people brag, 'I started with nothing, but because I worked hard and was thrifty, I got what I have today.' This implies that people are poor because they are lazy and wasteful; when the truth may be that poverty is the result of discrimination and economic exploitation. The poor often find themselves the victims of social injustice and psychological oppression by a society that equates their poverty with God's disfavour.

Protestantism versus Jesus

The value system of many Protestants is described by Max Weber as being diametrically opposed to the attitudes of

Jesus. He was a friend of the poor and the needy who heard him gladly because he gave them good news from the heavenly Father.

> Looking at his disciples, he said: 'Blessed are you who are poor, for yours is the kingdom of God. Blessed are you who hunger now, for you will be satisfied. Blessed are you who weep now, for you will laugh. Blessed are you when men hate you, when they exclude you and insult you and reject your name as evil, because of the Son of Man. Rejoice in that day and leap for joy, because great is your reward in heaven. For that is how their fathers treated the prophets. But woe to you who are rich, for you have already received your comfort. Woe to you who are well fed now, for you will go hungry. Woe to you who laugh now, for you will mourn and weep' (Lk 6:20–25, NIV).

Jesus was the incarnation of the eternal God who heard the cries of the oppressed children of Israel and championed their cause against the rich and mighty Pharaoh. Jesus was the same God who caused Amos to warn the rich people of Israel to beware of the Day of Judgement that would come upon them because of their indifference to the plight of the poor.

Jesus made it clear that wealth, instead of being proof of godliness, could easily be a barrier to a rich person hoping to enter the kingdom of heaven.

> Jesus looked around and said to his disciples, 'How hard it is for the rich to enter the kingdom of God!' The disciples were amazed at his words. But Jesus said again, 'Children, how hard it is to enter the kingdom of God! It is easier for a camel to go through the eye of a needle than for a rich man to enter the kingdom of God.' The disciples were even more amazed, and said to each other, 'Who then can be saved?' Jesus looked at them and said, 'With man this is impossible, but not with God, all things are possible with God' (Mk 10:23–27, NIV).

The wealthy person is in a very precarious position when it comes to entering the kingdom. It is hard to see how a person can live in luxury when so many of his brothers and sisters in the world live in degrading poverty.

John Wesley urged Christians to work as hard as they could, to make as much money as they could, in order to give away as much as they could. Wealth, even comparative wealth, is an awesome responsibility. Christians cannot escape the words of Christ: 'From everyone who has been given much, much will be demanded; and from the one who has been entrusted with much, much more will be asked' (Lk 12:48, NIV).

Pulling down the blinds

During a visit to Haiti, I went to a restaurant. The waiter seated me by a large window. He took my order and then brought me a very attractive dinner. I was about to eat a bite of steak when I happened to look to my left. Eight hungry Haitian children, with their noses pressed up against the glass, were staring at my food. I immediately lost my appetite and set the fork down. The waiter, seeing what was happening, quickly moved in and pulled down the venetian blind. He said to me, 'Enjoy your meal. Don't let them bother you.'

I thought to myself, *Isn't that what we all do? We pull down the blinds so we don't have to look at the poor and hungry of the world.*

I believe that God will punish our indifference to the poor. Our wealth, instead of being evidence of our blessedness, will be the cause of our judgement.

Reward in this world

I don't want to suggest that the only positive payoff for a Christian is life beyond the grave. While I do believe in heaven and on hell, let me say that even if these two realities did not exist, I would still be a Christian because of the reward that a commitment to Christ delivers here and now.

I cannot promise wealth, power, and prestige to followers of Christ, but I can say that those who sacrifice financially in his name are rewarded in this world. Those who forego the prestige that the world offers will be blessed in a manner that this world cannot understand. Christians who empty themselves of the need for power and become servants of others in the name of our Lord will experience a joy that knows no bounds.

Personal and Group Study Guide

For personal study

Settle into your favourite chair with your Bible, a pen or pencil, and this book. Read a chapter, marking portions that seem significant to you. Write in the margins. Note where you agree, disagree, or question the author. Look up relevant Scripture passages. Then turn to the questions listed in this study guide. If you want to trace your progress with a written record, use a notebook to record your answers, thoughts, feelings, and further questions. Refer to the text and to the Scriptures as you allow the questions to enlarge your thinking. And pray. Ask God to give you a discerning mind for truth, an active concern for others, and a greater love for himself.

For group study

Plan ahead

Before meeting with your group, read and mark the chapter as if you were preparing for personal study. Glance through the questions making mental notes of how you might contribute to your group's discussion. Bring a Bible and the text to your meeting.

Arrange an environment that promotes discussion

Comfortable chairs arranged in a casual circle invite people to talk with each other. It says, 'We are here to listen and respond to each other—and to learn together.' If you are the leader, simply be sure to sit where you can have eye contact with each person.

Promptness counts

Time is as valuable to many people as money. If the group runs late (because of a late start), these people will feel robbed as if you had picked their pockets. So, unless you have mutual agreement, begin and end on time.

Involve everyone

Group learning works best if everyone participates more or less equally. If you are a natural *talker*, pause before you enter the conversation. Then ask a quiet person what he or she thinks. If you are a natural *listener*, don't hesitate to jump into the discussion. Others will benefit from your thoughts but only if you speak them. If you are the *leader*, be careful not to dominate the session. Of course, you will have thought about the study ahead of time, but don't assume that people are present just to hear you—as flattering as that may feel. Instead, help group members to make their own discoveries. Ask the questions, but insert your own ideas only as they are needed to fill gaps.

Pace the study

The questions for each session are designed to last about one hour. Early questions form the framework for later discussion, so don't rush by so quickly that you miss building a valuable foundation. Later questions, however, often speak of the here and now. So don't dawdle so long at the beginning that you leave no time to 'get personal'. While the leader must take responsibility for timing the flow of questions, it is the job of each person in the group to assist in keeping the study moving at an even pace.

Pray for each other—together, or alone

Then watch God's hand at work in all of your lives.

Notice that each session includes the following features:

Session topic—a brief statement summarising the session.

Community builder—an activity to get acquainted with the session topic and/or with each other.

Questions—a list of questions to encourage individual or group discovery and application.

Prayer focus—suggestions for turning one's learning into prayer.

Optional activities—supplemental ideas that will enhance the study.

Assignment—activities or preparation to complete prior to the next session.

Chapter One: What is success?

Session topic

Even Christians are in danger of having the concept of success shaped more by culture than by God's word.

Community builder

1. When you were a child, what did you dream of being when you grew up? Were wealth, power, or prestige involved?
2. List the first five words that come to mind when you hear the word 'success'. What influences have shaped your view of success?

Group discovery questions

1. What role does Campolo see success playing in our lives?
2. What, in our culture, are considered the main ingredients of success?
3. Why is wealth often seen as an indication of success?
4. How is power often defined in our society?
5. What is prestige? Why do we seek it?
6. Campolo notes that many people mistakenly identify wealth as 'evidence of superior spiritual stature' (p.10). How does this distort the Judeo-Christian message?

7. Why is power so appealing to us? How does a craving for power affect our relationships with each other and with the Lord? What choices did Jesus Christ make in regard to his personal power?

8. How do you react to the statement, 'Those who seek prestige will never get it from God' (p.17)?

9. If Jesus Christ were living in your community today, would he be considered successful?

10. In what ways did the early church succumb to worldly standards of success? In what ways did they show a grasp of God's standards?

11. What do you think might be some of God's reasons for seemingly turning our definitions of success upside down?

12. Of the three supposed indicators of success—wealth, power, and prestige—which has exerted the strongest pull in your life? What dangers does that present for you? How have you dealt with it?

13. Though we might never be famous, each of us has some degree of wealth, power, and/or prestige. How might the Lord use those gifts in your life to further his kingdom? What hard choices might be involved?

Prayer focus

Ask the Lord to help you identify any faulty standards you have for judging success. Pray that his standards will become more and more a part of your outlook, and offer your portion of wealth, power, and prestige to the service of his kingdom.

Optional activities

1. Think of Christians you know who seem to be patterning their lives according to God's standards of success. Ask one of them what helped him or her to let go of worldly standards and choose God's standards. Share any

struggles you are having in that process, and invite his or her feedback and prayer support.

2. Make a chart with three headings across the top: Wealth, Power, Prestige. Under each heading, log any situations this week in which you notice yourself tempted to pursue that goal. Begin to notice the kinds of situations in which you are most vulnerable to worldly attitudes, and ask the Lord to strengthen you in those times.

Assignment

1. Memorise Matthew 6:33 and ask the Lord each day to show you specific ways to seek his kingdom and righteousness.
2. Read Chapter 2 of the text, and try to recall the kinds of success you have pursued and whose approval you culti-vated. (Try looking through old photo albums to jog your memories.) Work through the study for Chapter 2.

Chapter Two: Successful people can be disciples

Since our feelings of success are derived from the approval of 'significant others', we need to learn to turn to Christ as the ultimate Significant Other and to accept the success he gives us.

Community builder

1. Think of a compliment you have received that made you feel especially successful. In what ways did the identity of the compliment giver affect the significance of that feedback for you?
2. When you judge your own success or failure, through whose eyes do you tend to see yourself? Whom do you picture as your most significant evaluator? Why?

Group discovery questions

1. What makes people feel successful?
2. How is it that some people who have achieved a great deal continue to feel like failures?
3. What constitutes a 'significant other' in our lives. Who have been your significant others? In what ways are we influenced by our significant others?

4. Note that our choices of significant others change as we go through life. Why do you think this is so?

5. What role does competition play in our strivings and in our judgements of others? Is it healthy or unhealthy?

6. In what ways can accepting Christ as our Significant Other change our ideas of success and failure? What difficulties have you had in recognising Christ as your Significant Other?

7. List some of the paradoxes inherent in our acceptance by Christ.

8. Why is grace often difficult for us to grasp and accept? What has been your experience?

9. When we are 'tortured by the belief that we have not done enough to be worthy of his approval' (p. 24), what antidotes might we apply?

10. What practical steps can you take to disengage from seeking approval at the human level and to install Christ as your Significant Other?

Prayer focus

In prayer, name the persons or groups from whom you most commonly seek approval, and ask that the Lord himself will take the place of highest importance. Thank him for his willingness to be so intimately involved in your life.

Optional activities

1. During the week, notice and list the audiences to whom you find yourself playing. Note how this helps or hinders your walk with the Lord.

2. Team up with someone else working through this study. Share with each other the situations in which you are tempted to seek the approval of someone other than the Lord. Agree to pray specifically for each other in regard to those temptations, and get together with each other

at the end of the week to review progress and offer encouragement.

Assignment

1. During the week, keep in mind the ways in which the Lord has already given you his approval. Look for evidences of his approval each day.
2. Read Chapter 3 of the text, recalling your own childhood experiences. Work through the corresponding study.

Chapter Three: Successes and sufferings of little people

Session topic

When we give children the same acceptance that God gives us, we free them to become what God intended and to develop a healthy relationship with Jesus Christ.

Community builder

1. Recall a childhood achievement. How did the reaction of your opposite-gender parent affect your feelings about yourself and the event?
2. Write down the first five words that come to mind when you think of God. What connections do you see between your impressions of your heavenly Father and your experience with your earthly father?

Group discovery questions

1. Tony Campolo describes how young boys and girls look particularly to their opposite-gender parent for approval. When have you seen evidence of this? For what reasons might God have designed us this way?
2. Why might some parents withhold approval from their

children? What happens to children when they are unable to gain parental approval?

3. Read Ephesians 6:4. What does 'exasperate' (NIV) mean? (Compare with other Bible versions.) Why do we need this warning? Under what circumstances are we sometimes prone to be too hard on our children?

4. Campolo observes, 'The way God relates to his children is the best model for encouraging children to higher levels of achievement, without inflicting emotional hurt' (p.30). List some of the elements of how God relates to us. What personal experiences can you recall of God's fathering in these ways?

5. How can we practically demonstrate to our children some of what we have experienced of God as parent? Which elements do you find hardest to demonstrate to your children?

6. Why might Christian parents be especially tempted to take advantage of a child's desire to please?

7. In what ways are the children in your family different from each other? How can you guard against contributing to sibling rivalry?

8. How do you react to the authors' statement. 'What children believe, think, and feel about their heavenly Father will be highly influenced by what they think about their earthly fathers' (p.33)?

9. When you accepted Christ as Saviour, were there ways in which you experienced healing for childhood hurts? In what ways has your experience of your heavenly Father been better than your experience with your earthly parents?

10. All parents fall short of perfectly demonstrating God's love to their children. What implications does this spell for them? What are God's provisions for our shortcomings?

Prayer focus

Thank God for the special ways he has been a Father to you.
Pray for each of your children, asking God to help you to
accurately reflect his fatherhood. Pray that God will heal
them of any damage from your shortcomings.

Optional activities

1. List the traits and types of behaviour you appreciate in
   each of your children. Post the lists where you and your
   children can see them often.
2. Make a similar list about your parents.
3. Keep a log of your parenting experiences this week—
   whether as a child, a parent, or a parent figure. Note especially when you are reminded of God's attitudes towards
   you and are able to communicate similar attitudes to
   someone else.

Assignment

1. Talk with your parenting partner or a friend about an area
   in which you want to strengthen your relationship with
   your children.
2. Read Chapter 4 of the text and work through the corresponding study. If you don't have school-age children,
   take steps to familiarise yourself with the schools in your
   community.

Chapter Four: School daze

Session topic

The goal of education should be to foster each child's God-given capacities and thus contribute to a healthy sense of self-worth.

Community builder

1. What do you think constitutes a good education?
2. As you look back at your school days, what experiences were significant (either positively or negatively) in shaping the person you are today?

Group discovery questions

1. Campolo notes that for school-age children, approval from teachers can assume importance rivalling that from parents. Do you agree? Why or why not?
2. In what ways can the significance of teachers have 'potential for both good and evil' (p.38)?
3. What signs should parents look for to evaluate whether or not a child's schooling is going well?
4. What are parents' responsibilities in regard to their children's schooling?

5. In what ways is the 'process' of a child's education as significant as the 'content'? What effects can this have on children?

6. Make two columns on a sheet of paper. In the first column, list ways in which your community's school system perpetuates negative or destructive values. In the second column, list ways in which it contributes positively to children's growth. Note especially any ways in which the school system (either purposely or inadvertently) promotes biblical values.

7. Campolo describes the destructiveness of certain kinds of competition in schools. Why do you think this continues? What attitudes do you think Christians should take?

8. Read Ephesians 6:10–18. What are some ways in which we can wage war against the 'forces of evil' (NIV) in our schools? What might be some of the costs?

9. Do you see Christian schools as the solution to the country's educational ills? Why or why not?

10. If you were establishing a Christian school, what would be your goals? What elements would be necessary to achieve those goals?

11. What elements of the kibbutz schools described by the author appeal to you? What elements do you find undesirable? What principles can be drawn for our own educational system?

12. Reflecting on the author's comments and your own understanding of Scripture, how would you like to be affecting your community's school system?

Prayer focus

Thank God for the special gifts he has given each individual. Pray that your children (or children you know) will be able to develop those gifts in their schooling.

Optional activities

1. Listen carefully to the comments children make about school. Sometimes even the most offhand comments can yield important insights when explored. Talk with children to find out more about the positive and negative experiences they may be having at school.

2. Give yourself an opportunity for some direct contact with your local schools: visit or help in a classroom; volunteer as a parent helper for a special event; interview a teacher, administrator or school governor. What impressions do you form about what is happening there? What responsibilities for involvement do you see?

Assignment

1. Be alert to the educational issues in your community, and make them a focus of prayer and involvement.

2. Read Chapter 5 of the text and work through the corresponding study. Begin to familiarise yourself with your local teen culture.

Chapter Five: Coming of age

Session topic

Teenagers, anxious to find success by conforming to their peers, need the experience of true acceptance and affirmation through their identity with Jesus Christ.

Community builder

1. Did you enjoy being a teenager? Why or why not? How much of a role did acceptance by other teens play in your experience?
2. Most secondary schools have several different cliques or groups. What groups are predominant in your community's teen culture? What resulting pressures might teens in your community be facing? How are these similar to or different from the pressures you faced as a teenager?

Group discovery questions

1. Campolo observes that popularity among peers might become a teenager's ultimate goal. Why do you think this is so? What function does a peer group serve for the developing adolescent?

2. What do teenagers in your church need to understand or do to be 'in' with the youth group?

3. How might rejection by the peer group affect a teenager? Do you know of cases in which a young person was severely damaged by such a rejection? Are there cases when such rejection ultimately resulted in good for the boy or girl?

4. Do you agree with the author's statement. 'The church has always attracted society's losers because they can feel like winners within its fellowship'? Why or why not? If true, what are some of the positive or negative implications for your local church?

5. Campolo describes the 'other-directed personality' as one whose behaviour is motivated more by other's expectations than by personal conviction. Why are teenagers particularly susceptible to this? Are we as adults also susceptible?

6. Do you know any 'chameleons' (p.53)? What struggles might that person be experiencing?

7. Why is it difficult for teenagers to be individualistic?

8. Read Romans 12:1-2 in several translations. What is God telling us? How might a teenager respond to those verses? How do 'you' respond?

9. What difference can Christ make to a teenager struggling with peer pressure? How do you deal with peer pressure?

10. Discuss and expand on the author's statement, 'Christ is the source of true individuality' (p.56). In what ways have you experienced this in your own life?

Prayer focus

Pray for your teenager or another teenager you know, particularly in regard to peer pressure. Pray that the presence of Christ will have a stronger influence than the negative pressures in that young person's life.

Optional activities

1. Offer yourself as a mentor or prayer partner to a teenager you know. Teens often appreciate an accepting adult outside their immediate family with whom they can share freely.
2. Interview a youth group leader and/or teenagers in your church to find out what pressures are being faced by Christian teens. Make those concerns a matter of prayer, and look for ways you can help.

Assignment

1. Take note of ways in which you respond more out of other-directedness than out of true personal conviction. Remind yourself of Christ's acceptance.
2. Read Chapter 6 of the text and work through the corresponding study. Recall some of your own school dating experiences.

Chapter Six: Teenage success with the opposite sex

Session topic

Young people struggling for success with the opposite sex need to grasp the good news of Christ's acceptance of them just as they are.

Community builder

1. Drawing on memory or observation, have a male and a female group member role play a typical teenage first date. How do teenagers feel in that situation? How do they act? What are their hopes and fears?
2. What messages about relationships are today's teens getting from popular music and music videos?

Group discovery questions

1. Why do you think that dates are 'the ultimate status symbol' for teenagers?
2. Campolo notes that for teenagers, 'The dating game is played for stakes that are too high for most of us older folks to remember' (p.57). What do you remember about the importance of dating when you were a teenager? What do you observe in teens you know?

3. List some of the means by which teenage boys try to attract girls? What does the church have to say to these boys?
4. List some of the means by which teenage girls try to attract boys' attention? What does the church have to say to them?
5. What are some of the effects on the teenage boy or girl who is unsuccessful in 'the dating game'? What are some potential long-range consequences?
6. How can the negative effects of an unsuccessful dating career be redeemed or reversed?
7. What are some of the effects—both positive and negative—on teenagers who are successful in dating?
8. What particular temptations do teenagers face in dating?
9. What would you most like to say to the adolescent who is not dating much? The one who is heavily involved in dating?
10. What are some of the cultural messages you see aimed at teenagers today in regard to dating? What different messages does the church give to these young people? How can we counteract society's messages?
11. What is the church's responsibility to teenagers regarding the issue of dating? What practical measures can Christians take to meet their needs? How can you be involved?

Prayer focus

Pray for the teenagers in your church, especially in this difficult area of opposite-gender relationships.

Optional activities

1. Watch a TV show aimed at the teenage audience. What part does dating play in the show's plot? What messages are being conveyed to young people? If you have a teenage son or daughter, find out how they respond to such a show.

2. Find out ways you can influence the choice of social activities sponsored by your local secondary school or church youth group. What suggestions can you make for minimising the pressures of dating?

Assignment

1. Browse through some popular magazines aimed at teenagers to educate yourself further as to the kinds of messages and pressures teens receive from the non-Christian world.
2. Read Chapter 7 and work through the corresponding study. Try to identify some of your own attitudes and assumptions about midlife.

Chapter Seven: Symptoms of midlife males

Session topic

Midlife males need Christ's help not to follow false avenues of escape from midlife depressions.

Community builder

1. What are the first images that come to mind when you hear the term 'midlife crisis'? What is your attitude towards those experiencing such a crisis?

2. With markers on a large sheet of newsprint, draw a portrait of the 'typical' midlife male. (One group member may do the actual drawing, while the rest of the group suggests what they think should be included). Include features such as posture, weight, hair and clothing style, facial expression, and the activity he is involved in. Discuss the portrait you have drawn. How do you feel towards this man?

Group discovery questions

1. In what areas do men typically strive for success? Why do you think vocation has become so significant?

2. What are some of the differences between what a person 'is' and what he 'does'? Do these two areas ever overlap?

3. Campolo notes that Christians ought to be evaluating individuals according to criteria different from what the world uses. List some of the criteria you think Christians should be using, and, if you can, note Scripture references supporting your criteria.

4. In what ways can the church fall into the trap of loving things and using people? Why do you think this happens? How can it be avoided?

5. Make a list of Jesus' disciples and the professions they were involved in. (You will need to consult the Gospels as well as the text.) What does this tell us about Christ's choice of followers? What kind of 'job interview' do you think he used in his selection?

6. In what ways have you been influenced by our society's standards, both in your choice of work or career, or in your evaluation of others? What have you found helpful in combatting those influences?

7. How is it possible for Christians to have 'a deep sense of success, even when the world is unimpressed by them'?

8. Why are midlife men in our culture particularly vulnerable to midlife crisis?

9. How do current conditions (such as the economy and world events) affect today's midlife male?

10. What are some typical 'escape routes' chosen by men experiencing midlife depressions? What are midlife men looking for down each of these roads? Are these men's needs valid? What does Christ have to offer to those needs?

11. What do you think are the biggest dangers facing midlife males in your community? How would you like to see the church addressing these dangers? How can you be involved?

Prayer focus

Thank the Lord for his sovereignty and care over every stage of our development through life. Ask him to help you and your church to be sensitive to the needs of midlife men among you.

Optional activities

1. Redraw the midlife male portrait, this time with features that suggest that he has found contentment and confidence in Jesus Christ.
2. Write a response that you imagine Jesus might give to a man experiencing midlife crisis. What attitudes are reflected? What actions might Jesus take or recommend? How can 'you' reflect Christ to such a man?

Assignment

1. Choose an area of concern faced by today's midlife male, and look for Scripture passages that speak to the needs represented.
2. Read Chapter 8 and work through the corresponding study.

Chapter Eight: Hope for the forty-three- year-old man

Session topic

In Jesus, men in midlife crisis can find significance, security, adventure, and purpose.

Community builder

1. Describe a man you know (or know of from history) who changed his life radically in midlife. What motivated his change? How did it affect the quality of his life?
2. Have two group members stage a five-minute debate concerning security versus adventure. Then discuss which way you would cast your vote, if you had to choose, giving reasons for your choice.

Group discovery questions

1. What are some practical steps a man can take to avoid or mitigate a midlife depression?
2. Why is it important for a man to re-examine his life at midlife?
3. Campolo observes that sometimes distinguishing between what is 'really' important and what is 'relatively'

important can lift depression. Can you think of a time when such an evaluation lifted your spirits?

4. How can looking at your vocation in a new way promote a sense of success? How do you typically view your work? Are you overlooking some positive or commendable aspects of your work?

5. When might a change in occupation be called for? What are some pros and cons of changing jobs? What issues should a person who is considering a job change take into account. How can we discern God's will in such a change?

6. Campolo notes the tension between a need for security and a desire for new adventure as basic to our lives. How has this played out in your life? In what ways do you try to resolve this tension?

7. The author cites Abraham as a biblical model of someone who, under God's leading, made a radical change late in life. What other biblical examples can you think of? What lessons can you learn from them?

8. How does a commitment to Christ enable us to be adventurous? What adventures have you been able to embark on because of your security in Christ?

9. What are the primary elements that give our lives meaning? Why do you think relationships play such a big role?

10. How does a relationship with Christ give significance to your life?

11. What things does Jesus look at in evaluating our lives? What did you do today that he would commend you for?

Prayer focus

Thank Jesus that he is Lord over the turning points in our lives and that he gives meaning to even our smallest endeavours. Ask him to direct your steps to follow him more closely each day.

Optional activities

1. On a sheet of paper (A4 size or larger) draw a 'map' of your life, noting crossroads and turning points. Draw a symbol of Christ's presence at places where you especially sensed his support and guidance.
2. Choose a biblical character such as Abraham, David, or Paul. Do a study of his life, focusing mainly on the changes and challenges he faced in the second half of his life. What kind of choices did he make? What were the results?

Assignment

1. Draw up a list of people who add meaning to your life. Each day, plan one action designed to affirm at least one of those relationships.
2. Read Chapter 9 and work through the corresponding study. Reflect on your attitudes towards midlife women.

Chapter Nine: Pressures on the midlife woman

Session topic

Women in midlife face many pressures from society that undercut their God-given worth.

Community builder

1. Share with the group what you know of the roles your mother and grandmother played during their middle years. (If you can, show photos of them.) What is different for you or for midlife women you know?
2. What do you think is the most important issue facing midlife women today?

Group discovery questions

1. How have the roles of women changed over the past several generations? In what ways do those changes reflect social and economic changes in our country?
2. List some of the commonly held expectations for women today.
3. What part do husband and family play in a woman's view of herself?

4. What support systems are typically available for today's mother? What is missing? How does support or lack of support affect a woman's expectations and evaluation of herself?

5. What elements of sexism remain in our society? How does this affect a woman's view of herself?

6. List some of the concerns feminists have had over the past several years. What does the Bible have to say to these concerns? In what ways should Christians be speaking up regarding these issues?

7. What TV shows are most popular right now? How are women portrayed? Are there any women of middle age or older? If so, what kind of image do they have? If not, what message is contained in that omission?

8. Campolo cites the Roman Catholic stance that 'it is not the prerogative of society to define what a woman should be but rather the prerogative of God' (p.100). What are some similarities or contrasts between society's definitions and God's definitions of womanhood? What difficulties does a woman face if she resists ungodly societal expectations. How can you support women trying to live up to God's standards?

9. What 'games' do you see women playing? As a man or woman, how might you have been pulled into contributing to such games? How do these games detract from the personhood God intended for you?

10. What hopes do you have for changes in the roles and expectations of women? What would you like not to see changed?

Prayer focus

Thank the Lord for how he values women. Pray that he will correct any faulty views you hold. Ask him to help you give appropriate honour to women you know or to yourself as a woman.

Optional activities

1. Glue words and picture from magazines onto an A4 sheet of paper to make a collage 'mirror' that shows society's image of the 'ideal woman'. Then make another collage that gives a more biblical reflection.

2. Scan some current issues of parenting magazines. List the concerns or issues that seem to come up repeatedly in those magazines. What practical steps can the church take to meet the needs of today's mothers? Pray about ways you can be involved.

Assignment

1. Notice the ways the media impacts (or would like to impact) your view of women this week. Pray that the Lord will continually refine your views of womanhood.

2. Read Chapter 10 and work through the corresponding study.

Chapter Ten: Women, work, and the feminist movement

Session topic

Employment outside the home can be an important part of a woman's life and needs to be addressed by the church.

Community builder

1. What were your initial reactions when you read this chapter title? Where did those thoughts and feelings come from?
2. Have women in your family of origin generally worked outside the home, or did they stay at home? What have you chosen for your present family?

Group discovery questions

1. What are some reasons women today seek work outside the home?
2. List some of the problems women face (both external and internal) when seeking outside employment, particularly if they have never been employed or are re-entering the working world.
3. How has the feminist movement attempted to address these problems? How should the church be addressing them?

4 How does your church view the 'working mother'? What concerns are reflected in this view?

5. What would you like to see the church doing to address the needs of mothers?

6. What are some potential positive and negative effects on children when a mother works outside the home? How can parents work as a team to provide for their children's needs?

7. Who are some biblical examples of women employed outside the home?

8. How might a woman's self-concept be affected by her job? Give personal examples if possible.

9. How might a woman's self-concept be affected by her children's behaviour and choices? Give personal examples if possible.

10. Why do you think mothers are the ones most often blamed when children are having difficulties? Why do you think they are likely to accept such blame?

11. What would you like to say to a mother who is feeling guilty about her children's situation? What Scriptures would you offer her?

12. List some of the myths the feminist movement might perpetuate about caring for the home and about the working world. What kernels of truth might these myths contain? How can you keep a balanced perspective?

13. How can a relationship with God shape a woman's sense of identity? How do you work this out in your own life?

Prayer focus

Thank the Lord that he is the ultimate source of our identity and security. If you are a woman, ask him to help you strengthen that relationship and to make wise choices in regard to work and what needs to be the primary focus of your responsibility. If you are a man, ask him to help you see the woman in your life as he sees them and to be supportive of them in their fields of endeavour.

Optional activities

1. Survey some Christian women you know who work outside the home. What tensions have they faced? How have they coped with them? How has the church been supportive or unsupportive to them?
2. Clip out news or magazine articles that highlight tensions between stay-at-home mums versus those who have outside employment. List some ways the two sides might help rather than undermine each other.

Assignment

1. In your devotional reading this week, note and jot down scriptures that tell or show how God gives us our identity.
2. Read Chapter 11 and work through the corresponding study. Reflect on the differences between singleness and married life.

Chapter Eleven: Single people and success

Session topic
Single adults have special needs and challenges as well as unique opportunities for service and self-worth.

Community builder

1. If you are single, describe some of the current challenges you face. If you are married, recall some of the challenges you faced during your single years.
2. Who are some single Christians you know or know of (even from history or the Bible) who have had a significant impact in furthering Christ's kingdom? How has their singleness affected their ministry?

Group discovery questions

1. Campolo believes that society regards a happy family as a symbol of success. Do you agree? How can this be a misleading symbol?
2. From what groups or individuals do singles often encounter pressure? What are some of the messages these people give singles? How can you show sensitivity and respect to singles?

3. What are some of the reasons an adult might be unmarried?
4. From 1 Corinthians 7:7–9, 32–34, list some of the advantages Paul sees in singleness. Lost some of the challenges he identifies.
5. In what situations might singleness be an advantage?
6. What special difficulties might be faced by those who are single but not by choice?
7. How would you answer someone who sees his or her singleness as a failure of God?
8. What are some ways a single person can maintain or bolster his or her self-esteem?
9. What are some of the options for a single person's living arrangements? What biblical principles might apply?
10. Outline some ways a single person might manage his or her sexual feelings.
11. What are some of the stresses faced by those who are single through divorce? How can you help?
12. What attitudes do you see in yourself towards those who are divorced? How do you think Christ wants us to view those who have been divorced?
13. What are some of the arguments for and against a divorced Christian remarrying? How can the church transcend the arguments in its dealing with the remarried couple in its midst?
14. What responsibilities does the church have towards those who are widowed? What special ministries might they need? What special ministries might they have to offer?

Prayer focus

Thank the Lord for his sovereignty over the choices and happenings in our lives. If you are married, ask for graceful sensitivity to the single people you know. If you are single, ask for a vision of what your singleness might mean in terms of ministry and your own self-esteem.

Optional activities

1. Choose an unmarried character from the Old or New Testament, and write out what he or she might say if called on to be a guest speaker at your church.
2. Interview some of the singles at your church to find out what has been positive for them in giving and receiving ministry. Also find out if they have needs that are not being addressed by the church.

Assignment

1. Choose at least one single friend or acquaintance to remember in prayer this week (and let him or her know that you are praying!).
2. Read Chapter 12 and work through the corresponding study. Think about your own attitudes towards aging and the elderly.

Chapter Twelve: The throwaway people

Session topic

The church, as a representative of Christ, has a responsibility to honour the elderly and serve their many needs.

Community builder

1. How do you feel about growing old. Why?
2. How would you like to spend your retirement years?

Group discovery questions

1. What are some common social attitudes towards aging? On what are those attitudes based?
2. What does retirement mean in our society? Do you look forward to it?
3. List the gains and losses commonly experienced in retirement in our society. Which list is longer? What are the implications for an elderly person's sense of success?
4. Imagine that you are seventy years old. Where would you want to live? What are your options? Would you ever choose to live in a retirement home? Why or why not?
5. What are some of the needs of those who live in retire-

ment homes? What are the practical ways the church can minister to those needs?

6. How are the elderly treated in your church? Do you agree with Campolo's statement, 'The measure of our Christian love can be seen in the way in which we treat the elderly' (p.135)? Find some Scripture passages to support your answer. What responsibilities do you see for yourself?

7. List some ways the elderly can be active, significant participants in the life of the church. What do we miss when they are not?

8. What are some attitudes towards death in our society?

9. How do you think the relative nearness of death affects an elderly person's view of himself or herself?

10. How does your relationship with Christ affect your view of death? How does it affect your evaluation of yourself in the light of death? Are there any changes you need to be making in your attitudes or actions?

11. What would you like to hear Christ say to you as you meet him in heaven? What are some clues from Scripture as to what he might say?

12. What factors contribute to a person's being able to face death with a sense of success?

Prayer focus

Thank the Lord for his care and the honour he gives to the elderly. Ask him to lend you his perspective and guide you into productive paths as you age. Ask him also to help you find ways to minister to and honour the elderly people you know.

Optional activities

1. Using a concordance and the cross-references in a study Bible, explore the Bible's view of aging. Write a one-paragraph 'theology of aging'; use first person to make it personal.

2. Visit a retirement home. From talking with residents and staff, and from your own observations, list the particular needs represented there. Choose one area of need and plan an activity for yourself or your group that might contribute towards meeting that need.

Assignment

1. Plan a way to honour at least one elderly friend or relative this week.
2. Read Chapter 13 and work through the corresponding study.
3. Review Chapters 1 to 12 and think through any new understandings you have about true success.

Chapter Thirteen: A theology of success

Session topic

The success God offers us defies measurement by worldly standards of wealth, power, and prestige.

Community builder

1. Complete the following sentence: 'If there were no life after death, I would_____.'
2. What evidence do you look for to determine whether God is blessing your life?

Group discovery questions

1. What are some popular assumptions about the benefits of having faith in God? What scriptures can you think of that either support or refute those assumptions?
2. Campolo cites Will Herberg's observations that Americans have 'faith in faith'. What do you think that means? Do you agree? Describe a time when you fell into that error.
3. What are some common misconceptions about prayer? In what ways do they dishonour God or distort the gospel? Why do you pray?

4. Read John 15:18–21. In what ways might Christians today experience the world's hatred? What personal experiences have you had of being mistreated because of Christ's name? How can a Christian respond when this happens?

5. What scriptural evidence do we have for life after death?

6. What do you think it means that 'beyond the grave the " first will be last; and the last, first"' (Mt 19:30)?

7. Campolo states, 'For those who are in Christ there is a blessedness which transcends capitalistic value systems.' Name some examples of capitalistic values being confused with God's blessing.

8. What is the 'Protestant work ethic'? What are its strengths? What are its weaknesses? In what ways might we perpetuate some of the false notions inherent in that teaching?

9. How does the Protestant work ethic contribute to the oppression of the poor? How do you think Christ would have us view the poor?

10. From the Beatitudes quoted in Luke 6:20–26, list the conditions that Jesus called blessed. In contrast, what does our society call blessed? What tensions does this create for you?

11. Read Mark 10:23–27. Is it wrong to be rich? What dangers and responsibilities does a wealthy person need to be aware of?

12. What struggles have you worked through in regard to your attitudes about money? What conclusions have you come to? How have your actions been affected?

13. Having worked through this chapter as well as the previous chapters, how would you summarise your own theology of success?

Prayer focus

Thank the Lord for the presence and promise of his blessings, in both this life and the next. Ask him to give you a clearer vision of what it means to be truly successful and to help you make daily choices with eternity in view.

Optional activities

1. Compose a eulogy for yourself that reflects what you
   hope someone might be able to say of your life.
2. Write out a list of priorities that you would like to see
   governing your choices and goals.